Jean Joseph Languet, George Bernard Burder

Confidence in the mercy of God

Jean Joseph Languet, George Bernard Burder

Confidence in the mercy of God

ISBN/EAN: 9783742860255

Manufactured in Europe, USA, Canada, Australia, Japa

Cover: Foto ©Lupo / pixelio.de

Manufactured and distributed by brebook publishing software (www.brebook.com)

Jean Joseph Languet, George Bernard Burder

Confidence in the mercy of God

CONFIDENCE IN THE MERCY OF GOD.

BY

MONSEIGNEUR LANGUET,

ARCHBISHOP OF SENS AND MEMBER OF THE FRENCH ACADEMY.

TRANSLATED FROM THE FRENCH BY

THE RIGHT REV. ABBOT BURDER,

ORDER OF CISTERCIANS.

𝕻𝖊𝖗𝖒𝖎𝖘𝖘𝖚 𝕾𝖚𝖕𝖊𝖗𝖎𝖔𝖗𝖚𝖒.

LONDON:
R. WASHBOURNE, 18 PATERNOSTER ROW.
1876.

PREFACE OF THE TRANSLATOR.

THE valuable Treatise on Confidence in the Mercy of God, which is now presented to the English reader in an English dress, was written more than one hundred and fifty years ago. There are reasons which make me hope that this little book may, by the Divine Blessing, be of service at the present time, to the pious in England — both Catholic and Protestant. England is only just waking up to Catholicity, after its long sleep of three hundred years. Of course what is first needed is the Faith; but after that, I hesitate not to assert that what is most wanted by converts is a great confidence in the goodness and mercy of Almighty God. This confidence is necessary to feed and nourish their faith. It may be acquired by the habit of looking back, and of looking forward. In looking back a convert finds he has been passing long years, perhaps, in ignorance, and it may be, in sin. He has great need of confidence in that mercy which has permitted him to remain so long in darkness, and in the shadow of death, only to grant him, later on, the Divine light, and so to "direct his feet into the way of peace." The mercy of God, according to the Royal Prophet, is "from eternity." From all eternity, therefore, he has been chosen to become a true and living member of the Holy Church. This conviction feeds both his sorrow and his love—his sorrow for his sins, and his love for so good a God, Who has made choice of him from all eternity, to bestow upon him the infinite blessing of reception into the Church. The fruit, then, of this looking back is a great confidence in the mercy of God, and this confidence greatly nourishes his faith. Again, if he looks forward, the mercy of God is "unto eternity." In the hundred and thirty-fifth Psalm it is the refrain in each of its twenty-seven verses, "for His mercy endureth for ever." This truth makes him confide and firmly trust and hope in that mercy for the future, and this confidence gives him peace in trial, and strength in temptation, and so helps his faith. Unhappily a few of our converts have become apostates; but were they well trained in this holy confidence in the mercy and goodness of God? I think not. This looking back and looking forward are the two wings of faith—with them it is easy to fly up to heaven—but without them we cannot take an upward flight.

It has been remarked by a priest, who had charge of a mission in London, that he had been surprised to find, in the course of his pastoral labours, so many cases of despair. Whether the fact was owing in any way to the sombre character of the English people, to the nature of the climate, or to the continual inhaling of a saddening Protestant and unbelieving atmosphere, I know not; but it is clear that English Catholics have need of a great confidence in the mercy of God, of "that hope" by which, St. Paul says, "we are saved," and in consequence, sanctified. This excellent Treatise may, therefore, in this respect, do good. It is full of striking thoughts, of beautiful applications and explanations of the Holy Scripture; and it is written in a clear, logical, and forcible style. It cannot fail, by the Divine Blessing, of imparting to the devout reader, that "blessed hope" and confidence in God's infinite mercy, which makes our love of Him so tender as well as strong.

One word with regard to Protestants. This little work, if devoutly read, may show them, by God's grace, the true, interior, and most cheerful and loving character of our Holy Religion. A religion which steers so clear of both presumption and despair—which preserves so well the golden mean between these two extremes, and so beautifully and scripturally harmonises God's mercy with His justice—must be Divine. No human intelligence, no satanic craft could do this consistently and in detail. This Treatise, then, if read attentively by devout Protestants who love their Bible (if, indeed, such old-fashioned Protestants really exist now-a-days), must open their eyes to the truth I have just stated. When they see the Catholic doctrine of predestination, for example, so excellently unfolded out of the

Holy Scriptures, and so solidly and logically, as well as so simply, worked out from the writings of St. Paul, they must confess that the Catholic Church is the true interpreter of the Holy Scripture, and that the same Holy Spirit is the Author of them both, as we say in the Apostles' Creed: "I believe in the Holy Ghost," and then immediately we add, " in the Holy Catholic Church."

I have subjoined to this translation, in an appendix, a beautiful prayer of St. Mechtilda and St. Gertrude, on "Trust in God," which I earnestly recommend to the use of the readers of this Treatise, especially to those who are inclined not to confide sufficiently in His infinite goodness and mercy. It is taken from the Prayers of St. Gertrude, published by Burns, Oates, and Co., London. Also I have added in the appendix, by the kind permission of the Very Rev. Canon Vaughan, O.S.B., a chapter from "The Spiritual Conquest." This chapter is entitled "Confidence in God's Goodness is the main support of our Spiritual Edifice." The whole chapter is a kind of an unconscious epitome of the Treatise of Archbishop Languet.

I gladly take this opportunity of strongly recommending "The Spiritual Conflict and Conquest," edited by the pious and learned canon, as an invaluable digest of the entire spiritual life.

Abbaye de St. Marie du Désert,
    Par Lévignac,
        Haute-Garonne,
            France.

FEAST OF ST. BENEDICT,
  March 21st, 1876.

ADVERTISEMENT OF THE EDITOR ON THE EDITION OF 1859.

THE inestimable author of this little Treatise, published it for the first time in 1718. Several editions have been printed, and some since the Revolution. We wish to remark that every subsequent edition is like the first; also that this work, though written with purity, and even eloquence of style, is not well known, nor has it been sufficiently circulated. Yet there are few Treatises that would be found more useful to the faithful generally, but especially to the timid and distrustful; more fit to preserve them from discouragement, to make them taste the delights there are found in the service of God, and to nourish in them those sentiments of confidence which sweeten all our inferior pains, and make the most painful crosses seem light and easy to bear. It is, then, to those who are easily discouraged in the way of virtue, who are troubled at the remembrance of their sins, and whose hearts the judgments of God fill with too great a fear —it is to such, in particular, that we offer this Treatise. The doctrine it contains is pure and solid, and the style in which this little work is written is superior to what is usually found in works of a similar kind.

CONTENTS.

FIRST PART.

IN WHICH ARE LAID DOWN THE FOUNDATIONS OF THE CONFIDENCE WE OUGHT TO HAVE IN THE MERCY OF GOD.

CHAPTER	PAGE
I. The Mercy of God is little known, particularly by those who give themselves up to Fear	1
II. The Different Sources of this Fear	6
III. What kind of Fear it is which is spoken of in this Treatise. There is a Fear which is Useful and Necessary. The Fear that is condemned is excessive Fear	10
IV. The Bad effects of excessive Fear. The First is Discouragement	13
V. The Second consequence of Fear. Sadness of Heart; the peril of this State	17
VI. The Third Effect of excessive Fear, the weakening of Tenderness in the Love of God. First, it is proved how necessary this Tenderness is. First Proof	22

CHAPTER		PAGE
VII.	Second Proof of the Tenderness our Love of God ought to have. It is Confidence which Excites these Sentiments of Tenderness	27
VIII.	The Tenderness of our Love of God is Destroyed by Distrust and Fear	34
IX.	Continuation of the same Subject. The Difference between Two Persons, one of whom is Governed by Love and the other by Fear. Portrait of the First	39
X.	Portrait of another Just Person who is Governed principally by Fear	43
XI.	Those who are Conducted by Love and Confidence are more agreeable to God, and their Lives are more according to the True Spirit of Christianity	47
XII.	Other Proofs of the preceding Truth. Three solid Grounds for our Confidence. The principal Ground is the Goodness of God	51
XIII.	The Goodness of God is more touching in His tenderness for Sinners	58
XIV.	Not only is this Confidence established on a solid Foundation, but it appears to be an indispensable Obligation. The care God takes to excite it in us	65
XV.	It is to do an Injury to God to refuse Him this Confidence which He asks of us	70
XVI.	Other characteristics of Confidence in the Mercy of God. The five Advantages we find in it	74

CHAPTER	PAGE
XVII. The sixth Advantage of this holy Confidence—it gives us a great Consolation in our Difficulties and Troubles	80

SECOND PART.

IN WHICH THE OBJECTIONS SUGGESTED TO THE TIMID BY FEAR ARE ANSWERED.

I. Objections of the Timid and Scrupulous. First Objection, the strict and severe Justice of God. Description of the Severity of His Judgments	85
II. Reply to the first Objection. How Terrible soever God is, He is still more Amiable. What advantage it is for us to have Jesus Christ for our Judge	90
III. Continuation of the same Subject. Jesus Christ is the most favourable of all Judges. First, because He is full of Goodness, and Kindness	97
IV. Secondly. Jesus Christ is a Judge full of Compassion	101
V. Thirdly. Jesus Christ is at the same time our Judge and our Friend	103
VI. Fourthly. Jesus Christ is a Judge Who is interested in our Salvation	107
VII. Fifthly. God is a Judge Infinitely Just; it is precisely because He is so Just that we ought to hope in Him	112
VIII. Continuation of the same Thought. Another reason proves that even the Jus-	

CHAPTER		PAGE
	tice of God ought to strengthen our Confidence - - - - - -	117
IX.	Second Objection of the Timorous; the greatness and the multitude of their Sins - - - - - - -	122
X.	Reply to the foregoing Objection. The Sentiments of God towards the Sinner are the Sentiments of Mercy; He Loves him, and is moved with Tenderness towards him, in that he is a Sinner -	125
XI.	God Calls the Sinner, and even His threats in Calling Him should rather excite our Confidence than discourage our Weakness - - - - -	133
XII.	Confirmation of the foregoing. Image of the Tenderness with which God seeks the Sinner, according to a History related by an Ancient Author (Valerianus Maximus) - - - -	138
XIII.	God having spoken in Vain, Mercifully condescends to wait still longer for the return of the Sinner. How admirable this Patience is; the Consequence he ought to Draw from it -	142
XIV.	Fourthly. Almighty God receives the Sinner with kindness the moment he returns to Him - - - - -	149
XV.	Continuation of the same Subject. How God receives Sinners. Parable of the Prodigal Son. Image of our Misery in this libertine - - - - - -	155

CHAPTER		PAGE
XVI.	Continuation of the same Parable. Image of the Goodness of God in that of the good Father who received his Prodigal Son - - - - -	162
XVII.	The fifth Characteristic of the Goodness and Mercy of Almighty God towards Sinners in receiving them, He Pardons them - - - -	168
XVIII.	Sixthly. God not only Pardons the Penitent Sinner, but He appears to Favour him more than the Just -	174
XIX.	Conclusion of the same Subject. To be too alarmed about our Sins, is sometimes a Refinement of Self-Love	178
XX.	The last Objection of those who are Distrustful—the small number of the Elect; general Reflection on this Truth - - - - - -	181
XXI.	Another Reflection on the same Truth. Confidence in God is a Means of assuring in some sort our Predestination	185
XXII.	Principal Reply to the Objection mentioned in the preceding Chapter. The small number of the Elect is a consoling Truth for those who have reason to think they belong to this small number. What are the Marks of Predestination. First Mark, Choice and Vocation - - - - -	191
XXIII.	Second Mark of Predestination. Conversion and Particular Protection -	195

Contents.

CHAPTER		PAGE
XXIV.	Third Mark of Predestination. Perseverance in Grace. Reasons for hoping it. Proofs of Predestination taken from the Temptation itself to Discouragement - - - -	200
XXV.	Who those are who have the most certain Marks of Predestination. It is they who are in Affliction - -	207
XXVI.	Proofs of the preceding Truths. First, it is in Sufferings that we find the truest Vocations - - - -	214
XXVII.	Second Proof. It is in Suffering that we find the surest Expiation of Sin. Advantages of Involuntary Afflictions above Voluntary Penances -	221
XXVIII.	Third Proof. In Afflictions we find the most certain Means of avoiding Sin for the future - - -	225
XXIX.	Fourth and Last Proof. Affliction forms in us the Likeness to Jesus Christ. This Likeness is the Consummation of Predestination - -	229
XXX.	Recapitulation or Abridgment of all that is contained in this Work -	234
XXXI.	Conclusion of the Treatise. We Confide in God for temporal things, we must Confide in Him also for our Salvation and our Predestination -	239
APPENDIX	- - - - - - -	242

A TREATISE

ON

CONFIDENCE IN THE MERCY OF GOD.

FIRST PART.

IN WHICH ARE LAID DOWN THE FOUNDATIONS OF THE CONFIDENCE WE OUGHT TO HAVE IN THE MERCY OF GOD.

CHAPTER I.

THE MERCY OF GOD IS LITTLE KNOWN, PARTICULARLY BY THOSE WHO GIVE THEMSELVES UP TO FEAR.

Of all the perfections of God made known to us by reason and by faith, there is not one which we think we know so well, but of which actually we know so little, as that of His infinite mercy. We think we know it well, because we talk of it continually, it enters into all the reflections we make on the eternal truths; and it is the soul or motive of all our sentiments of piety. If it ought to be the consolation of the just, it would seem, particularly in our day, that it should be the comfort and the support of repentant sinners. Yet, I say, that we do not know the mercy of God, or that we know it, as it were, only by halves, and that we do not form a just and worthy idea of it. I say this, principally in the case of those who make use of it as a sort of prop to their wicked life, who continue to be wicked because God continues to be merciful, and who reckon upon His mercy to warrant their continuance in sin; this state of mind is a common one—it has been so at all times; and the Holy Scripture often condemns the rashness of the presumptuous. There are others, however, who appear more enlightened, and who are so in truth, but in this matter, they have not light enough. Far from presuming too much on the goodness of God, they know the full extent of the obligation they are under to work out their salvation, and in truth, they labour for that end—they labour too with courage, they have no attachment to the world and its pleasures—they fear sin even to scruple; they are exact in fulfilling the duties of their state; and they give the better part of their time every day to prayer, and to the practice of works of charity. Yet in the midst of these holy, occupations the thought of the mercy of Almighty God gives them no consolation whatever. Struck with the terrible thought of His judgments, and of His justice, they forget what a God-man, a God-infant, a God-Saviour, a God-spouse has in Him of amiability; they only occupy their minds with the thoughts of what a God-judge, a God-avenger, has in Him of what is terrible. Hardly do they dare to hope in Him. The thought of the divine love, which to others brings so much sweetness, gives them only disquiet, and the fear of not loving Him enough.

They are afflicted, they are in trouble, their desolate heart tastes in the practice of virtue neither sweetness nor repose. We may say that if in sinners confidence becomes presumption, we may find also in some who are just, so lively a fear, that it becomes discouragement.

Many times have I seen these fervent Christians abandon themselves to this fear, of which I am now speaking, and I could not help compassionating their anxieties. I have also seen some of whom I cannot speak without alarm, who, too weak to make head against their scruples and their fears, have fallen into a dreadful state of dejection and despair—and why? Because in the fear they had of the justice of God, they had forgotten the confidence with which His mercy ought to have inspired them, and which would have given them encouragement and support in the time of trial. I have seen others, who deriving from the same source another kind of error, and discouraged with a piety which cost them so much disquiet, abandoned entirely the practice of the Christian virtues, in order to seek, in the false freedom of the world, the peace they had not found in the service of God.

The error into which such persons have fallen, came, no doubt, from the fact that they did not know how to measure, according to the rules of Christian prudence, the limits of the justice and of the mercy of God—they did not know either their measure, or their extent. Far otherwise was it with the Royal Prophet, who chanting alike the praises of both these divine attributes, both of God's mercy and of His justice, found in His justice a reason for that fear which is the "beginning of wisdom," and in His mercy, for that confidence which is the consummation of charity. "Mercy and justice I will sing to Thee, O Lord." Ps. c. 1.

If the want of confidence in God is an afflicting temptation during life, it is still more saddening at the approach of death; at that hour the mind is weak, and "the corruptible body presseth down the soul," which can then hardly support the lively impression of this fear. It is then, however, that we naturally feel this fear the most, because the judgments of God appear most terrible, when we see them, as it were, close at hand. If during life their remembrance alarms us even to discouragement, how shall we be able to bear the thought of them, at the hour of death, without despair? Thence came often those disquiets, those agitations, those repugnances, that we sometimes remark, with astonishment, in the just, who have lived in fervour, and whom we are surprised to see die in sadness and desolation. But this sadness is not caused by any attachment to life; there is no other reason for it, than an immoderate fear of the judgments of God, without the assurance of hope. St. Hilarion is not the only one who has had need to seek, in long years of penance, wherewith to comfort his timid soul, which seemed, at the hour of death, to hesitate to leave his body to go to God, whose judgments he so much feared.

CHAPTER II.

THE DIFFERENT SOURCES OF THIS FEAR.

THESE fears and alarms seem to be the same in all those who experience them. However, in many cases, they have different sources. In some, they come from pure ignorance; they have not considered, nor taken the measure of God's justice, nor of His mercy—they have not known the nature of Christian hope, much less have they understood the nature of that confidence, which is the fruit and perfection of this virtue. Tenderness of heart, and the consolation it produces, the ordinary effect of this confidence, is likewise equally unknown to them. Finally, what they are still more ignorant of, is the intimate connection of confidence with the fervour of charity, which should find therein its sweetness and its consolation.

Those who are better instructed, and, consequently, more enlightened, are not always exempt from similar fears. In their case, these fears come from the temptation of the demon, who, not being able to seduce the just by the excess of confidence with which he deceives so many, endeavours to seduce them in an opposite way, and to throw them into discouragement and despair. He does this by exaggerating the inexorable severity of the divine judgments, or by heaping up before their eyes the number and enormity of their past sins, or by reproaching them for their daily faults, filling their minds with scruples, or by representing to them the imperfections of their good works. These evil spirits, who, as Holy Scripture saith, "are created for vengeance, and in their fury lay on grievous torments" (Ecclesiast. xxxix. 33), at the approach of death employ their utmost violence against the just, and against those who are in mortal sin. It is at the hour of death that they make their last efforts to throw them into despair. They know that this is the only means left to weaken the charity of the just, or put an obstacle to the conversion of sinners.

We may find a third source of these excessive fears, in the Will of God, all tenderness as He is for those who are in the state of grace. He is pleased sometimes to alarm them with the view of His judgments, and instead of consoling them with the remembrance of His mercies, He seems to withdraw His mercies from them, and even to abandon them. He deprives them of His sensible Presence, and the consolations of His love, in order, by these rigours, to test their courage and their perseverance. It is thus, in the Canticle of Canticles, the Spouse hides Himself for a time to prove the fidelity of His Beloved, and perhaps, also, that she may taste the greater sweetness in the joy of finding Him again.

Such is the experience of the Saints in times of dryness and interior privations, of fearfulness and desolation, when the soul thinks herself almost abandoned. It is the state so well described by all the masters of the spiritual life, and by the Royal Prophet, who owed so much to the mercy of God, but who was not the less sensible to all the terrors of His justice. Now whether they are caused by ignorance, by temptation, or by trial, it is always important to console those who are troubled by their fears, which are often excessive, always dangerous, and sometimes a sad source of relaxation. For if confidence, through pride, is carried to presumption, it is not surprising that fear, through timidity, should lead to discouragement and despair.

CHAPTER III.

WHAT KIND OF FEAR IT IS WHICH IS SPOKEN OF IN THIS TREATISE. THERE IS A FEAR WHICH IS USEFUL AND NECESSARY. THE FEAR THAT IS CONDEMNED IS EXCESSIVE FEAR.

WE must remark, however, that it is only excessive fear that we would condemn, and not fear itself; for it is true to say that there is a salutary fear which is not only "the beginning of wisdom," and its foundation, but which ought always to remain in the heart of the just, to support them in every position of life, and to accompany them in all the degrees of perfection. It is indeed the want of this fear which keeps so many in tepidity, who think themselves just, though they are not really so, because the evil one has seduced them by presumption, by illusion, and by pride.

We may add, that there are holy and chosen souls, walking in the way of piety, who go to God by the road of fear; they are faithful to God, precisely because they fear Him. Their fear, it is true, is not that servile fear, which has in it no mingling of love, or but a very slight impression of it: it is a fear which supposes love, but which is stronger than love, as to its sensible impression. I would compare it to the love of those children who, by the austere conduct of their parents or superiors, acquire by education a natural timidity. Although they love their Father, they are always, while in His presence, in some apprehension and alarm. They think that He only looks at them to punish them, and that He speaks only to reprove them; they have for Him all the sentiments of love which nature has given them: but the tenderness and sensibility which their love ought to have, are stifled by their too lively impressions of fear and timidity.

Such is the disposition of those of whom I speak. They love God, but they are more conscious of fearing than of loving Him—and it is good that they are conducted by this road; for it is only this lively fear that can restrain a heart naturally presumptuous, or humble a mind that swells every moment with vanity. Hence it comes that Almighty God makes the most fervent feel these impressions of fear and alarm, in order to keep them, by this means, in holy humility, and to repress the pride which would otherwise be excited by the abundance of graces they received. Far from condemning these dispositions, I admire the goodness of God, Who condescends to abase Himself, in order to study, so to speak, our individual character, to accommodate His graces to our wants, and adapt them to our weaknesses.

I pray Him, with all my heart, to grant this spirit of fear to the presumptuous, who dishonour devotion by their proud confidence. But I do not write this Treatise for them, nor for those who take advantage of the mercy of God to persevere in their impenitence—there are books enough both for the one and for the other; it depends on themselves to profit by them. It seems, indeed, in these last days, that greater care is taken to intimidate the faithful by setting before them all that is severe and terrible in the judgments of Almighty God, than to give them comfort and consolation; but if it is necessary to alarm, it is necessary also to inspire confidence and love, and since fear has its defects, its excess, and, consequently, its dangers, it must also have its remedies.

CHAPTER IV.

THE BAD EFFECTS OF EXCESSIVE FEAR. THE FIRST IS DISCOURAGEMENT.

I SAY that fear has its dangers, and I reckon the first to be the discouragement that it entails on those who give way to its impression. It begins by trouble and agitation; then comes bitterness, and the soul falls into sadness. From sadness to discouragement there is but one step, and this is a slippery one. It is very difficult, in this lowness of spirits, to resist the temptation which urges us to abandon a road in which we see nothing but what affrights, and where we gather nothing but thorns.

How, in truth, in the midst of all the bitterness which an excessive fear can inspire, how are we to bear, at once, all the restraint we have to put on our senses, the yoke of an exact fidelity, the severity of penance, and the austerity of a hard and painful life? Man, according to the thought of St. Bernard, cannot live on this earth without consolation, and if he is not held up in the path of virtue by some sweetness and consolation, it is difficult for him to bear, for any length of time, its necessary restraints. "The unction of grace," says St. Bernard, "is necessary to help our infirmity; the crosses of penance and of our religious practices must be anointed, because neither without the cross can we follow Christ, nor without unction can we support its bitterness."—(St. Bernard, 1st Sermon on the Dedication of the Church.)

It is true that this constraint and all the rigours of penance, are nothing to him who loves, who hopes, who tastes all the sweetness which the vivacity of love and the tenderness of confidence can give him. But if our heart is full of fear, if we have but a timid love, if we do not know the sweetness that is found in confidence in God, alas, how are we to be pitied! It is the most trying state we can imagine, and a penance the least supportable!

Thus we often see, that those who are the

victims of sadness, and who are devoured by scruples, seek again, sooner or later, in dissipation and in sensual pleasures the consolation they could not find in a life of piety, because all they knew of that life, was its austerity, its self-denial, and its fear.

I say further, that this fear of which I speak not only leads to discouragement, but it begets it; it produces it, by the weakness it causes in him who feels it. In ordinary enterprises, confidence is one of the means of success; at least it animates, and gives us fresh strength. Timid soldiers are already half conquered; on the contrary, the confidence with which well-trained troops enter the battle redoubles their ardour, and strengthens their courage. If it is so with success in human affairs, how much more in those that are divine, and in the great battle of salvation? For not only is salvation for us, soldiers of Christ, a kind of assault or combat in which we can only conquer by making great efforts, but confidence is an essential element of success. "We are saved by hope," according to St. Paul (Rom. viii. 24). In truth, if in human enterprises our confidence often deceives us, it is not so in the great affair of our salvation.

It is true to say that no one will be saved without hope, and that hope, or confidence, is one of the most effectual means of working out our salvation. "Hope confoundeth not," says St. Paul (Rom. v. 5). If, on the contrary, confidence is banished from the heart, what will you do with a heart full of timidity? A soldier discouraged is, as I have said, already half-conquered, because he fears being so; he would fly before the enemy because he does not think himself strong enough to resist him. He will be like those Israelites in the desert, the figure of the Christian people, who, by their fatal timidity, typified those who are discouraged by fear. Sometimes they were afraid to hear the voice of God, and they could not bear it. "Let not the Lord speak to us lest we die" (Exod. xx. 19). Sometimes they were disheartened at the sight of the armed chariots, and the warlike air of the people with whom they had to combat. "We cannot go up to the mountains, for the Canaanites have chariots of iron" (Josh. xvii. 16).

It is thus that these fearful souls of whom I speak, weakened by their timidity, are affrighted, sometimes at the obstacles they find in the way of virtue, and sometimes by the severity of the judgments of God, so that they soon sink under a weight which they think they are unable to support.

CHAPTER V.

THE SECOND CONSEQUENCE OF FEAR. SADNESS OF HEART ;—THE PERIL OF THIS STATE.

IF fear does not go so far as discouragement, at least it will produce sadness of heart. Now this sadness is enough to make fear perilous, if not fatal to the soul. To be convinced of this, I will show how this sadness is injurious to God, Who ardently desires that we should serve Him with a heart gay and content, and Who demands that the offerings He receives at our hands should be seasoned with this joy and contentment of heart.

"God loveth a *cheerful* giver," saith St. Paul (2 Cor. ix. 7). "How shall I appear before God," said of old time the Holy Pontiff Aaron, "how shall I please the Lord in the ceremonies, having a sorrowful heart?" (Lev. x. 19). He said this, in order to excuse himself from offering the sacrifice of his ministry in a time of mourning. In truth, nothing is less agreeable to a father who loves his children with tenderness, than to see them always in sadness, and responding to his caresses only by fear, seriousness, and silence. Almighty God, Who holds in our regard the title of Father, and Who, by His tenderness, to use the noble expression of Tertullian, is more a Father than all the fathers of the earth, does He not wish that we should answer to His caresses by confidence and joy?

I might also show how this sadness is injurious to piety, of which it gives to the people of the world a frightful idea, and disgusts them with it. For what must a man think, who knows neither the sweetness of virtue, nor the joys of penance, when he sees in those who live a holy life, an austere exterior, a wrinkled brow, a sombre look, a heart agitated by scruples which never end, and a mind overwhelmed by sadness, which seems to have no idea of God, but of His terrifying justice, and whose talk is always of His threats? Is not this enough to make the people of the world who see and hear him, reject for ever a piety which appears so sad and painful?

I do not, however, stop to consider further these two proofs; I limit myself to what more particularly regards my subject. I am speaking of that weakness produced by fear on the hearts of those who yield themselves to it with excess, a weakness that sadness necessarily increases. I wish for no other proofs than those that are furnished by the Holy Scripture itself. "By grief of mind," says the wise man, "the spirit is cast down" (Prov. xv. 13), and again, "drive away sadness far from thee, for sadness hath killed many" (Ecclesiastes xxx. 24), and again, "as a moth by a garment, and a worm by the wood, so the sadness of a man consumeth the heart" (Prov. xxv. 20).

If the fear and sadness which this weakness of the soul produces are so serious, I may say fatal, during the time of health, when they are both of them moderated by so many circumstances, how greatly will they be intensified at the approach of death. Then, fear and sadness will be more lively than ever, by the nearer presence of the objects that excite them; and then the demon exerts his utmost fury to strengthen the impression they make! Can I have enough fear for these sad and frightened souls, whose scruples have devoured them during life, who have never tasted the consolation of confidence, and who are filled with trouble at the thought of God's infinite justice? I cannot, I say, have fear enough, when I see them on the bed of death, because they need a special grace to deliver them from the temptation of despair. For then, for these over-timid souls, what new subjects of alarm and perhaps of discouragement, when they see, all at once, all those sins of their past life, each one of which has furnished inexhaustible matter of trouble and scruple! when they call to mind all their failings, and the infidelities of which they have been guilty, the sacraments which they believe they have received unworthily; the graces which they think they have abused; the omissions of which they deem themselves culpable, and of which the demon augments the enormity and the number! What a shock when they see close at hand those judgments of God which, when remote, appeared so terrible, and which certainly are a thousand times more so, when we are on the point of feeling all their rigour, when we touch them so to speak, with the hand, and when we look upon them as ready to overwhelm us! Experience teaches that there is the greatest difficulty imaginable, of tranquillising, at that time, even those who are very holy, and even those who have had the liveliest sentiments of confidence in the mercy of God—what will become, then, of those who have had all their life no other thoughts of God but of alarm and terror, who have been nourished with no other food than the bread of bitterness, and who have known little else of Almighty God but His judgments, and His severity? Will they not cry out with the Jews of old in their discouragement, "our iniquities and our sins are upon us, and we pine away in them—how then can we live?" (Ezech. xxxiii. 10).

CHAPTER VI.

THE THIRD EFFECT OF EXCESSIVE FEAR, THE WEAKENING OF TENDERNESS IN THE LOVE OF GOD. FIRST, IT IS PROVED HOW NECESSARY THIS TENDERNESS IS. FIRST PROOF.

SUCH are some of the sad effects that excessive fear produces, when it is not moderated by the consolations of hope, when no care is taken to join inseparably the remembrance of the mercy of God, and of His justice, and to sing with holy David alike the praises of both these attributes, of which the wise admixture on the part of God in His Church, constitutes the whole economy of our salvation: "Mercy and judgment I will sing to Thee, O Lord" (Psalm c. 1).

But this is not all the evil that excessive fear can produce: I will now explain another of its evil consequences, but little known, but which is no less real—it is the weakening in us of the love of God, which has never the vivacity it would have, if it was nourished with the tenderness of confidence, because I maintain that the surest means of attaining the perfection of this heavenly virtue of the divine love, is to feel all that hope has in it of sweetness. It is confidence that gives in part to love its vivacity, its fecundity, its consolation, and its tenderness. Examine what is the nature, the extent, the effect of Divine love in a heart which it inflames. Few people have the idea they ought to have of it.

We accustom the faithful to have sublime ideas of religion. We teach them to reason on it without end, even on the love of God, but we do not teach them to know this love. Never did we hear more of the obligation of loving God, and perhaps never did we know less of one of the beautiful characteristics of the perfection of this love;—this characteristic consists in its *tenderness*. Persons of the world know the fatal tendernesses of human love—but as to the tenderness of divine love, in our age, even pious and devout people seem to know nothing of it, and those who pique themselves on their elevated ideas, count it as a weakness, or as simplicity—yet it is the character our love of God ought to have. I establish this by two convincing proofs; the first is, that our love is a love of gratitude, and which answers to that which God has had for us from all eternity, and to that of which Jesus Christ has given us in time; our love, consequently, for God, should resemble God's love for us, and should equal it, if that were possible. At least, it ought to be modelled on the dispositions, so to speak, God has had for us.

How I love to represent Almighty God such as He is described in the Holy Scriptures, sometimes as a father, who carries his son in his arms, and in order that he might be continually in his sight, promises to carry him always, without tiring of his burden, which becomes the more heavy by his son's ingratitude; "hearken unto Me, O house of Jacob ... who art carried by My bowels, and borne up by My womb—even to your old age, I am the same, and to your grey hairs I will carry you. I have made you, and I will bear, I will carry and will save" (Isaias xlvi. 4 and 5).

Sometimes as a nurse or mother who presses her infant to her breast, and without being irritated by its importunate cries, caresses and embraces it, and exhausts herself to nourish it;

"Can a woman forget her infant so as not to have pity on the son of her womb—and if she should forget, yet will I not forget thee" (Isaias xlix. 15).

"I was like a father to Ephraim—I carried them in my arms, and they knew not that I healed them" (Osee xi. 3).

Sometimes it is a shepherd, who is afflicted at having lost the sheep he cherished, and who fatigues himself in seeking it. "He goeth after that which is lost, till he find it—and when he hath found it, he layeth it on his shoulders rejoicing" (St. Luke xv. 4, etc.).

How I love to read in the Holy Writings the sweet invitation of this God of goodness, Who presses us to give Him all our love. "My son, give me thy heart" (Prov. xxiii. 26).

He asks only for the tenderness of our heart; and in order that we may merit it, He offers us first His own, and all the love of which He is capable! If the inquietudes of love prove most effectually its vivacity and its tenderness, He has deigned to give us the description of what He feels, when He calls us, and when He awaits our reply, He asks us Himself, have

I done enough for you? "What more could I do for my vineyard, that I have not done for it?" He says it, as uttering a complaint in the hearing of all creatures, He calls them to witness His anxious care—He tells them in confidence His inquietude, He complains amorously of the little success of His love, and of our slowness to love Him. "And I sought among them for a man that might set up a hedge, and stand in the gap before me, in favour of the land, that I might not destroy it, and I found none" (Ezech. xxii. 30).

Oh how amiable is a God, Who thus bewails! When He could hurl the thunderbolt, He is contented to utter only a complaint. His complaints, and even His reproaches prove as much the tenderness of His love, as do His benefits and His caresses. For myself I own it is difficult not to be touched with them, even to tears, especially when I see the Son of God weep with tenderness for us, and over us. He beheld, says the Gospel, the city of Jerusalem, and He saw in it a figure of the Church which He came into the world to establish; He saw also in this city an image of the state of our hearts, which He wished to gain—immediately His love made Him shed tears over it, and at the same time over each of us—He weeps bitterly over our insensibilities—He weeps from affliction at our wanderings—He weeps with compassion over our difficulties—He weeps with disquiet over our combats—He weeps with joy at the crowns we gain—He weeps because a father cannot withhold his tears, when he sees again a son whom he loves and whom he thought to be lost. Such is the love of our God; a love which would answer by its gratitude to such paternal affection, ought it not to have the same tenderness? If the Prodigal Son had not mingled his tears with those of his father, would he have been worthy of so kind and merciful a reception?

CHAPTER VII.

SECOND PROOF OF THE TENDERNESS OUR LOVE OF GOD OUGHT TO HAVE. IT IS CONFIDENCE WHICH EXCITES THESE SENTIMENTS OF TENDERNESS.

THE second reason for tenderness in our love of God is that our love of Him is not only a love of gratitude, but also a love of complacency, such as ought to exist between husband and wife, for this is the rank which God gives to our soul, and the title and character He wishes to take in its regard. Now what ought this love to be, if not a love of the heart, which should exhaust all its desires and all its affections? How can we except the tenderness of the heart from the fulness of its love? What do I say? is it not in this tenderness of the heart that we find its most delicate sentiments, and, consequently, what is most perfect in the divine love?

Now this is true of all mankind, but principally it concerns those whose hearts are the most lively, and who feel most easily all the impressions of tenderness which love or friendship is capable of inspiring. Is it possible, then, that they should be sensitive in regard to creatures, and that they should dispense themselves from being so in their love of God? We are so tender towards a friend, a father, a benefactor; a mother is so tender towards her son, and a wife towards her husband!

The presence of what we love opens and dilates the heart; it swims then in joy; it is content; it is transported. Absence causes complaint, disquiet, and weariness, it imparts a bitterness even to life's most delicious pleasures; danger increases this disquiet, and nothing can calm it. Loss changes it into despair: we sigh, we are afflicted, we refuse our food, we will not occupy ourselves with anything else, but to weep and bewail our loss. I recognize in these characteristics the tenderness of the heart, and the vivacity of the love with which it is filled. Why is it then that this heart, so sensitive, so impressible with regard to creatures, has not the same love for God, or that the love of God does not produce the same effects?

It appears to me that if our heart is capable of feeling and cherishing this tenderness, we cannot be excused for being without it. Would it not be shameful to be so alive to earthly objects, and to have for our God a love without sentiment, and a heart without tenderness. I know not even if such a love is worthy of its name, or whether it should not rather be regarded as a real indifference.

It is, then, necessary for us to have this tenderness for our God, at least to desire it, to excite it, to labour to acquire it. What means are more fit to produce it, than the sweet confidence we should have for Him, Whose goodness we know, and Whose mercy we experience every day? What method more pressing to excite the sentiments of which I am speaking, than to say to oneself, "I have in God a good Father, Who loves me with tenderness; He is preparing for me an infinitely rich inheritance, and this inheritance is no other than Himself. In spite of my miseries and of my weakness, He wishes to make me holy, happy, and eternal as Himself. He knows, it is true, all my wanderings from Him, but He bears with me, in His goodness He excuses my wanderings, he dissembles His knowledge of them, and, all just as He is, it seems to me that for myself, He is still more merciful than just."

It is thus that St. Paul excited in himself these tender sentiments when he said: "I know in Whom I have believed; I know His goodness, His fidelity, His mercy, and I am certain that I shall not be deceived in my confidence." Then his love, animated by this motive, thought itself strong enough to bear even the hardest trials; he defied the whole universe to separate him from the love of his God, that love with which he was so transported. "Who," he cries out, "will separate us from the love of Christ?" (Rom. viii. 35).

Confidence ought to produce in us the same effect and the same sentiments. It produces them naturally wherever we find it. I am certain of the fidelity of my friend; and when I think of the marks of friendship he has shown me on certain trying occasions, of the help I have received from him—when I consider the assistance he has promised me in times of future difficulty, I feel my attachment to him redouble, and my whole heart empties itself, as it were, in the affectionate sentiments I have for him.

I am sure of the goodness of my father, and when I see the rich inheritance he is preparing for me, the cordiality with which he speaks to me, the amiability with which he instructs and corrects me, the facility with which he receives me, even after my wanderings from him, my tenderness for him is redoubled.

I am certain of the affection of my prince, and when I think of the words so precise, in which he has spoken to me of my future fortune, when I see his care to grant me the favours which occasionally offer, and that he often anticipates my wishes as a proof of his good-will, I feel my zeal and fidelity in his service twice as great. I would go to battle, in the thickest of the fight, to an assault full of danger, to prove to him my affection, and I think I cannot love too much, nor do too much for, one who is so good.

It is thus, that with far greater reason, when I think of what my God does for me, what He can do, what He has promised to do, what He gives, what He excuses Himself for not giving, what He has already given, what He will give me before long: I find myself inflamed with a new ardour in His service. It is to this point that my confidence in His goodness inspires me to go, and if I found in myself the least coldness in His regard, I have but to think of His mercy, in order to cover myself with confusion, and to renew in me His love.

It was thus that St. Ignatius, the martyr, thought and felt—that divine man, who knew so well the characteristics and the strength of the holy love with which he was inflamed. Writing to the Magnesians, he congratulated them that they manifested the full extent of their love for God and for Jesus Christ, in the greatness and the liveliness of the hope they had in Him. In truth, it is this merciful goodness of our God which gives to our love its sweetness and its force, and it is the confidence with which it inspires us, that disposes us to love Him more feelingly and with greater tenderness.

Therein, in this holy confidence, is that small quantity of leaven of which the Gospel speaks, which quickens the whole mass, and gives to it its taste and its excellent quality. "The kingdom of heaven is like to leaven, which a woman took, and hid in three measures of meal, until the whole was leavened" (St. Matt. xiii. 33). Therein, in a word, is that spirit of adoption, spoken of by St. Paul, which we have received in Jesus Christ, which teaches us not to tremble as slaves, but to love as children, to invoke our Father with confidence, to serve Him without disquiet, and to await in peace the food with which his tenderness supplies us. "For you have not received the spirit of bondage again to fear, but you have received the spirit of adoption of sons, whereby we cry, 'Abba, Father'" (Rom. viii. 15).

CHAPTER VIII.

THE TENDERNESS OF OUR LOVE OF GOD IS DESTROYED BY DISTRUST AND FEAR.

SUCH is the true spirit of Christianity, and such is its perfection. But what does the tempter do? Whether he would throw the just into trouble, or retain the sinner in sin, or cast the dying into despair, he does his utmost to destroy this holy confidence in every heart, that he may rob them of all the holy fruit it bears.

To the timid, he represents with exaggeration the multitude of their faults, the enormity of their sins; he suggests to them innumerable scruples as to every confession they have made, he troubles them by the most frightful temptations, and makes a crime of thoughts the least deliberate.

Discovering to them how strict and severe are the judgments of God, he endeavours to persuade them that their sins are beyond pardon, that Almighty God, irritated by their infidelities, refuses them His grace, that He abandons them in His anger, and that they are among the number of the hardened and the reprobate.

If these timid souls should hear of any threat or reproach, addressed in general to impenitent sinners, the tempter says to them interiorly, that it is to them these words are addressed, that it is for them these chastisements are prepared. If they hear any words of consolation, he adds to such consolations saddening reflections, and despairing thoughts, which hinder these souls from applying them to themselves, or from deriving from them any fruit. If they are sufficiently faithful to resist the temptation to despair, to which he urges them, he succeeds, at least, in troubling them, and throwing them into disquiet and a mortal sadness. Thus these poor timid souls, tempted, agitated, and desolate, do not know what part to take, seeing nothing before them but objects of fear, and in themselves nothing but monsters and darkness.

It is easy to see how this distrust, and this sadness of heart, furnish an obstacle to the vivacity and the tenderness of the love of God, such as I have described it. But how would I reason with those who abandon themselves to these sad and dangerous thoughts? I would say to them, "All your sadness comes from your distrust of the mercy of God, in which you dare not hope."

This distrust can come only from a doubt as to where you are, that is, in Whose keeping, or as to the almighty power of God, or His good-will in your regard. You cannot hesitate to believe in the power of the Almighty, and that your salvation is not difficult to Him.

Your doubt and your fear arise from your want of belief in His good-will towards you. You hesitate to believe that He wishes to save you; you fear that He will never pardon you; you think that He does not love you as much as others whom He has saved; you imagine His mercy is exhausted in your favour, and has given place to justice and to vengeance What fatal effects have such doubts and such thoughts on the love that ought to reign in your heart—for the most pressing motive for your love of God ought to be, that this God of love loves you. Yes, He loves you, sinner as you are, miserable as you are. He has manifested His love for you in calling you, in receiving you, and in pardoning you.

For myself, it is this thought that affects me the most, which touches me the most keenly. If I was a saint, if I was perfect, if I was just, it would seem that I had less reason to admire Your love. But what astonishes me, and what increases my love for You, and my gratitude, is, that in spite of my miseries, You love me still—it is that, sinner as I am, ungrateful and unfaithful, that I am still, in this state, the object of Your solicitude and of Your benefits. It is this which softens my heart; it cannot any longer resist such goodness.

Such are naturally the thoughts of a heart sustained by confidence in God. But what will become of these loving sentiments in him who falsely thinks, that it is in vain he loves his God Who is irritated with him, and has only His severity and His chastisements in store for him—that his sins have reached their full measure, and that they will never be pardoned! must he not fall into despair, to find in these sad thoughts the final decay of love? Is not the mere doubt of the infinite goodness of God sufficient to trouble, to sadden, to chill the heart, in proportion as it feels the diminution of its confidence?

CHAPTER IX.

CONTINUATION OF THE SAME SUBJECT. THE DIFFERENCE BETWEEN TWO PERSONS, ONE OF WHOM IS GOVERNED BY LOVE AND THE OTHER BY FEAR. PORTRAIT OF THE FIRST.

IN order to see more clearly the truth we have just stated, and to give it all the fulness it demands, and that we may feel it more sensibly, let us consider the difference that exists between two of the faithful, both just, if you will, but who go to God by different roads, the one by the way of confidence, and the other by that of fear.

The one loves God cordially and tenderly, as a son loves his father, or as the wife loves her husband. His love increases his confidence, and his confidence nourishes his love. "God is good," he says, "and He is my Father, and it is this which teaches me not to offend Him. But if I fall into any infidelity, I have recourse to Him with confidence, because I know that His mercies are greater than my ingratitude. I know that He is terrible in His anger, but I know also that His anger is not proof against a contrite and humble heart. It is just to fear Him, but He appears to me to be more amiable than terrible. I have experienced a thousand times that He pardons easily whoever invokes Him, and I shall never despair of putting Him again to the test. In spite of my feebleness, He will sustain me by His grace. This grace has been merited for me by the Blood of my Saviour, and in order that I may have a more abundant share in it, I will hide myself in His wounds, and I will clothe myself with His merits."

Such a one, in these sentiments, in order to please God, lives a life austere and painful, but his austerity does not show itself in his temper; he is gay, happy, and agreeable in society. His virtue has nothing in it of melancholy, and the tears of his contrition are mingled with a sweetness that makes them amiable. He loves to approach the sacraments, and especially to receive the Holy Communion. He finds it a joy he cannot express, thus to possess his God, Whom he loves, and to unite himself intimately to Him. Indeed it is with confusion that he approaches the Holy Altar, knowing how great God is, and seeing nothing but misery in himself. But this confusion does not stop him, because his fear yields to his love, and he believes it is more according to the Heart of his Spouse. This fervour sustains him in the most difficult occasions, and in the greatest temptations. He advances with giant strides in the way of God's commandments; he runs in them with enlarged heart [according to the expression of the Royal Prophet, "I have run the way of Thy commandments, when Thou didst enlarge my heart" (Ps. cxviii. 32)], in those thorny ways in which so many others find difficulties and dangers. What makes him run thus lightly and swiftly, is the holy joy with which his confidence animates him—this joy enlarges his heart and transports him; it raises him up even to God, borne on the wings of confidence and love, and from the height of his elevation he despises the world and its attractions, the devils and their trickeries, nor does he feel the weight of nature nor that of concupiscence.

This holy ardour redoubles at the remembrance of death. "Alas!" he cries, "my God, and the God of my heart, when will the time come for me to see You without a veil, when I shall possess You wholly, when I shall praise You without interruption, when I shall love You without tepidity? Burst, O Lord, the bonds which keep me from you, 'bring my soul out of prison,' and take me from a life in which I am always offending You, and can only half possess You."

The approach of death, naturally so alarming, only serves to inflame his fervour. "Ah!" he cries out, "my exile is about to end. I shall then enjoy the possession of my God, and repose in His bosom; my heart, freed from its prison, and liberated from its slavery, will see what no eye of man hath ever seen, and shall enjoy that happiness which no human heart has been able to conceive. Oh, my God and my Father, hasten that moment which can never come too soon for my desires! I know that Your justice will find much in me wherewith to be angry, much for which I deserve punishment, but I unite myself to Jesus Christ, by Whom You have saved me, and in Whom I love You. It is only in His merits that I place my confidence, and not in my own works, which of themselves are nothing worth; it is through His Blood that I ask Your mercy, and that I hope to obtain it."

In this sweet hope he abandons himself to all the pains of his sickness, and with this holy confidence in God he receives the last stroke of death which consummates his sacrifice.

CHAPTER X.

PORTRAIT OF ANOTHER JUST PERSON WHO IS GOVERNED PRINCIPALLY BY FEAR.

THE other just man, of whom I am now to speak, is a very different person. He wishes to love God, and in truth he does love Him: but unquiet in his love, he does not dare to say to himself that he does love truly. Carefully keeping before him all the faults he has hitherto committed, and his possible daily imperfections, ingenious in making fresh sins, subtle in the refinements of scruple, he exaggerates each of his defects, either those he has, or those he thinks he has—he forgets the mercy which forgives, and thinks only of the justice which punishes them—God is, for him, a God irritated, a terrible God, he lives with Him not as a child with a good father, or as a virtuous wife with an amiable husband, but as a servant with a master, a master who is hard and irascible, who sees all, and who forgives nothing. In truth, he walks with fidelity in the ways of salvation and of the commandments of God, but it is with sadness and sluggishness and fear.

Every moment he stops to forecast temptations, which sometimes he brings upon himself, because he fears them, and he makes them stronger by fighting with them. There is no victory which does not furnish him with a thousand different scruples. He does all at a cost—all is painful to him, because joy does not sustain him.

In this state he can hardly make up his mind to approach the sacraments—convinced of his unworthiness, he imagines that, instead of purifying himself by them, he is guilty of profanation. He trembles every time he presents himself in the tribunal of penance, he troubles his conscience as to the examination of his sins, the way he is to confess them, the quality and degree of his contrition, and puts his mind on thorns in its efforts to take every possible precaution. His scruples, which never come to an end, make of his conscience a terrible chaos, where he sees nothing in himself but darkness. The Holy Communion alarms him no less, and it requires all the authority of an able director to oblige him to approach his God, but his fright often gains the mastery over obedience, and the fear of irritating God by his unworthiness, which is always before him, hinders him from going to this God of goodness, notwithstanding His sweet invitation and the pleasure He takes in being united to us. These troubles and fears increase twofold at the thought of death. He has hardly any other idea of God but that of His justice and His vengeance. He knows that it is a terrible thing to fall into the arms of His wrath, and he regards with terror the moment which is to bring him before such a God. His alarms redouble the nearer this moment approaches; he would remove it from him, not by any attachment to life, but because he regards death, the end of life, as the awful entrance into eternity, where he sees nothing but fire and punishment, which he thinks are destined for himself.

It is easy to see that these two portraits I have just drawn are not ideal ones. We may recognise in the first a great multitude of saints, whose transports, whose fervour and tranquillity, astonish us when reading their holy lives—perhaps many devout and timorous persons may recognise themselves in the second. But whatever may be the application, it is just to draw the conclusion I had in view.

I do not ask which of these two states is the happier, and whose lot is the most sweet, but I ask which of the two is the more perfect—namely, he who loves the most, who is transported by that charity which "casteth out all fear" (1 John iv. 18)—or he whose fear is greater than his charity.

Which of these two spirits is the more conformable to the spirit of Christianity, that spirit of which St. Paul says, in the passage we have already cited, "we have not received the spirit of bondage again to fear, but you have received the spirit of adoption of sons, whereby we cry Abba, Father." In a word, I ask which of these two states is the more glorious to God, and the more agreeable to Him—which is more according to His Heart? can we doubt that it is that of the first I have described? God does not demand anything of us, but the dispositions of tenderness, of joy, and of confidence.

CHAPTER XI.

THOSE WHO ARE CONDUCTED BY LOVE AND CONFIDENCE ARE MORE AGREEABLE TO GOD, AND THEIR LIVES ARE MORE ACCORDING TO THE TRUE SPIRIT OF CHRISTIANITY.

LET us judge of what we have said by the ideas which nature herself gives us, and let us decide the matter according to the dictates of reason. Which of the two characters should we prefer ourselves, if it was a question of employing them in our own service? Should we not prefer the one who was full of affection and fervour, to the other who approaches us with sadness, and who would serve us only from fear? Whom should we love the most, the one who made himself loved, or the other who made himself feared? To what does the most noble ambition incline us? Is it to attract to ourselves a forced respect, exacted by fear and by terror? No! a voluntary homage inspired by love, and dictated by gratitude, appears to me to be infinitely more precious. He who would be able to captivate all hearts, would be, in my opinion, more worthy of admiration, than he who would subdue all nations. If the famous conquerors of whom history speaks, have made it their ambition to become the masters of the world, by force of arms, it was, without doubt, because they found it impossible to conquer it by the charms of love.

This is what reason itself dictates to us—but this same reason, enlightened by faith, should it not make us understand that our God, infinitely more equitable than ourselves, finds it more glorious to Himself to gain our hearts by love, than to subdue them by fear? In truth, this God of mercy, Who could oblige us to serve Him, has been so good as to content Himself with inviting us to do it, to press us, and to attract us by the sweetness of His love.

"He has given up," says St. Peter Chrysologus, "the title of Master, to take that of Father, because He would rather reign over us by love than by power."

He takes then the name of Father, and if this title has something in it too much of majesty, He adds that of Spouse, that of Friend, that of Saviour—He gives Himself to us under the appearance of simple bread, and He has shown Himself to man under the appearance of an infant.

Let us reflect a moment on this last thought, on the form that the Son of God took when He came on earth, and we shall readily see what is the principal disposition with which He wishes to inspire us, whether that of fear, or that of confidence. If He had come to chastise and to terrify, would He have taken a form so sweet, so feeble, so simple, so amiable? Would He have shown Himself as an infant, a little infant, who can do nothing without the help of its mother, an infant who has nothing but charms and sweetness—a poor infant, naked, abandoned, who moves us by its tears, and utters cries capable of piercing the heart of a savage? Alas! it appears to myself that He makes these cries heard only to complain that we do not wish to love Him, though on His side He makes so many advances—He hides, He disguises, He covers up, so to speak, all that He has of grand and terrible. He strips Himself of all that might appear inseparable from His greatness, His glory, His riches, His power, and His majesty. It is easy to recognise His design, He wishes to attract us to Himself, and make every one approach Him, He wishes to give us confidence, He wishes to annihilate all our distrust and our timidity—He wishes to make our access to Him so free, that there can be no excuse on our part for standing at a distance from Him.

Such then is the design of God in our regard; and consequently what He demands of us, is our love, our tenderness and our confidence. Judge then who it is that best answers to His designs, who enters the most into His views, and who has the dispositions that are the most agreeable to Him. Is it he who is timid, who is alarmed, and who cannot tranquilize himself without difficulty?—or is it he who is full of a respectful confidence, who loves Him, and who, humble in his love, tastes all the sweetness which tenderness always finds in that love? For my own part, I think that the tribute we ought to pay to His grandeur and to His Majesty is fear, but the offering we should make to His goodness is our confidence and love, since our God shows Himself to us as a God Whose goodness makes Him so amiable; it is therefore with love and with confidence that we ought to approach Him.

CHAPTER XII.

OTHER PROOFS OF THE PRECEDING TRUTH. THREE SOLID GROUNDS FOR OUR CONFIDENCE. THE PRINCIPAL GROUND IS THE GOODNESS OF GOD.

LET us proceed to throw a new light on this truth; and in order to discover more and more clearly the true spirit of Christianity, with regard to this confidence of which I am treating, let us consider carefully, still further, all those reasons by which we may better know its price, its solidity, its necessity, its advantages, and especially the consolation which inseparably accompanies it, and which constitutes, so to speak, its proper character. After this, it will be easy to remove the doubts of the timid, and to answer their objections.

Let us consider, then, first, the solid foundations of this tender confidence with which I would inspire all the faithful.

What are these foundations? They are, the infallible truth of God, His Almighty power, His infinite Goodness;—can our confidence find foundations more immovable? "Cursed be the man who trusteth in man," saith the Holy Scripture (Jeremias xvii. 5). Among other reasons which render such a one accursed, we may say that it is the imprudence of this trust, which leans upon too frail a foundation, and must disappoint his vain hopes. For what good or what help can we expect from him who fails almost always either in fidelity, or in will, or in power. Such is man here below. His heart is full of lies and malignity. Rarely does he wish to do good—he promises it, but his promises are false; he is unfaithful to them.

If he wishes it sincerely, it is but feebly; if he wishes it with fervour, he has no constancy; and when he would do good, and wishes it sincerely, fervently, and constantly, even when he is willing to give himself all manner of trouble in order to succeed, often his good-will is unfruitful. He exhausts himself in vain desire, because his power is too limited; it does not follow his heart, and if his friendship has no limits, his power is so confined, that he cannot do much for him whom he loves. What folly, then, to put our confidence in man, from whom we can expect such little real aid, and when we most want it!

Now what man wants, what he has not, this we find only in Almighty God. He is the truth eternal, unchangeable, and infallible, Who is as far removed from lies as He is from nothing; and Who promises what He carries out with more magnificence even than He has promised. A power which has no bounds, which everything obeys in heaven and in earth, and even in hell; Who changes the elements and annihilates His creatures, if he wishes, and Who holds the world in His hand, to use the noble expression of the Holy Scripture.

In the midst of the Majesty which this infinite power raises so high in our estimation, we find a heart full of tenderness for us, Who has for us a love as infinite as is His power, and which makes us experience all that love can invent of benefits to enrich us, and of mercy to pardon us.

"Three things," says St. Bernard, "animate my hope: the truth of God, which makes me promises; the power of God, which renders easy the execution of His promises; and the charity of God, which has adopted me to be His child. The truth of God, which promises me all the riches that this adoption bids me hope for; the power of God, which these rich gifts cannot impoverish; the adoption of God, which gives me the right to expect them, to demand them, and to obtain them" (St. Bern. de Diligendo Deo).

I do not stop here to consider what regards the truth and the power of God, the first foundation of our hope. The just man and the sinner, who never doubt them, would derive little benefit from the care we might take to convince them, either of God's truthfulness or of His power. It will be more useful to speak of His goodness, which we know in general, but which we do not meditate and consider sufficiently. But, shall I attempt to fathom this goodness and this mercy? Is it not an ocean which has no bottom, and the limits of which are far beyond our power of vision? Would it not be rashness to try to exhaust it?

What shall I say of the production of all those creatures which God has made to supply our wants, and which He has created even for our amusements and for our pleasures? "Not only," says a Father, "has He provided for our necessities, but He has deigned also to provide for our gratification" (St. Peter Chrysologus). What shall I say of that continual Providence, which by a thousand admirable contrivances preserves us, sustains us, protects us, and arranges favourable moments for our salvation? What shall I say of that admirable redemption by means of a God-man, in order to render us happy by His tears and by His sufferings, to procure us rest by His labours, to give us life at the expense of His own, and, let us say boldly with St. Leo, in order to make us share in His divinity, to place us on His own throne, and to make us, so to speak, so many gods?

These benefits are common to all mankind—they are prepared for all; but they do not the less manifest the goodness of God. On the contrary, it is in this very respect that we see more clearly the infinite extent of His goodness, which does not exclude entirely even the hardened and the ungrateful from those helps which He wishes to bestow upon all, because He loves us all. In other respects, common as are these benefits, they are in one sense particular in regard of each of us, as if there were none on the earth but ourselves to profit by them.

The love which has prepared them for us is a personal love, which, separating us off, as a shepherd, who calls each of his sheep by the name he has given it, loves us each in particular, as if there was no one else for Him to love. Yes! without doubt, whatever the Creator has of grandeur, whatever Providence has of consolation, whatever the Almighty has of riches, whatever eternal recompense has of magnificence, whatever the redemption, the sufferings, the blood, the death of Jesus Christ, have of tenderness,—all this belongs to us, and belongs in particular to each of us, as if there were no one else in the whole world but our own solitary self!

This is what deserves, I do not say our astonishment and our gratitude, these terms are too common for benefits so great, but our ravishments, our transports, our ecstasies! O that I could find stronger words, and more full of meaning, which would express the sentiments answering to so great a goodness!

CHAPTER XIII.

THE GOODNESS OF GOD IS MORE TOUCHING IN HIS TENDERNESS FOR SINNERS.

THE impossibility of conceiving all the greatness of so many benefits, obliges me to speak of them only in general. There is one thing, however, one benefit, concerning which I cannot be silent. It is that continual goodness with which Almighty God seeks and brings about the conversion of the sinner. He seeks him; He gives him a particular call, as if there were no one else in the world whom He wished to convert. He awaits him, He receives him, He pardons him. It is this continual, and, so to speak, this individual and personal mercy, which I can never be weary of admiring, and which ought to interest and engage our hope and our confidence.

What is it to love man, if not to call him, to seek him, to caress him, and to heap benefits upon him in the time even of his wanderings and of his sin? Is this not to carry tenderness as far as it can go? That Almighty God should love mankind, whom He has created, this seems just; they are His creatures, and the work of His hands, and on this account they can, so to speak, merit His attention. That He should love them, fallen as they are from the state of innocence, and in that state of misery to which they are reduced by the sin of their first parents—in that state which is owing to their fall—alas! they are in this state more worthy of pity than of anger, and I am not surprised that a God of goodness has sentiments of compassion in their regard.

But that men, not only sinners by their origin, but who, by a continual malice, add contempt to their crimes, and insult to contempt, who abuse the benefits of God, to make war against Him, who make His patience their warranty to increase their rebellion and their insolence; that men, in this state, should be the object of God's tenderness—that He should love them, that He should suffer for them, that he should caress them, that He should load them with His blessings—this is what God alone can do, and what man cannot comprehend.

And it is this that the author of Ecclesiasticus is never weary of admiring. "It is true," he says, "that in a certain sense we may say that the mercy of God to sinners has its limits, since He has determined the duration of their life, which does not go beyond 'at the most, a hundred years' (Ecclesiast. vii. 8), and that in thus fixing the number of their days, He seems to have prescribed strict limits to the period of His mercy."

But he wishes, in another way, to make us feel all its infinite extent, by the infinite abundance of graces with which He loads us in this passing life. He does not give us a certain part only of His mercy, but He pours it out all entire, so to speak, and with profusion. He hastens to anticipate the moment, which, in terminating our life, would begin in us the reign of His justice. He presses us as if He feared to be taken by surprise. In spite of our rebellions, He does not cease to love us, to support us, to call us, and to shower down on us His blessings and benefits.

He dissembles because the time is short, and He wishes that each moment of our life should be distinguished by some fresh mark of

His mercy. However, He is not ignorant that our ungrateful and proud heart will take occasion from His goodness to nourish its presumption and to justify its malice. He sees it, He is witness to it, because He penetrates all the secret folds of our soul, and He discerns all its corruption. "He has seen the presumption of their heart, that it is wicked, and hath known their end, that it is evil" (Ecclesiast. xviii. 10).

So unworthy a spectacle should tire His patience, yet His patience is not discouraged, and from our filled-up malice He takes occasion to fill up the measures of His infinite mercy. "Therefore hath He filled up His mercy in their favour, and shall show them the way of justice" (Ecclesiast. xviii. 11). Instead of our malice irritating His anger, it only excites His compassion. In His goodness He disputes with this ungrateful creature, and He hopes always to vanquish him by His caresses. We are proud, He humbles us—we are insensible, He softens us—we are in chains, He bursts our fetters—we fly, He pursues us. There is no time, no place, no occasion, no disposition, of which He does not profit, to make us hear His voice. In proportion as we take our steps of rebellion to remove ourselves from Him, He takes His steps of mercy to approach nearer to us.

Behold what the wise man admired! but it is only what we experience every day. Let us say it to our confusion, behold the portraiture of the obstinate rebellion of our heart, and that of the infinite mercies of our God. But though I feel them every moment, although every sinner feels them as myself, yet it is what neither I nor any other sinner can comprehend.

"What, then, is man," may I not cry out with the prophet, "what, then, is man, O my God, that you should treat him with so much care, and crown him with so many benefits?" "What is man that Thou shouldest magnify him, or why dost Thou set Thy heart upon him?" (Job vii. 17). What is man in himself? a nothing—whose life is a breath; a mass of corruption drawn from nothing, and whose lot is the dust, with a mind light, fickle, inconstant, full of ignorance and darkness. But what is man in Your regard, O my God? an ungrateful rebel, who having been Your enemy even before his birth, has willed a thousand times by his own malice to return to the state of rebellion in which he was born, and from which You had drawn him.

Is it he, then, O my God, is it such a being as man whom You have made the object of Your solicitudes and Your care! is it in him You place Your love and Your tenderness! But was it not enough in his miserable state to be the object of Your compassion? Yes, doubtless, it was enough for us—and yet He has made man the object of His caresses and of His complacency. It is this goodness of God which astonishes me, and moves me more than all His other acts of mercy. Is anything more wanted to excite in us the most lively confidence? at these remembrances, then, what will become of all our timidity and our distrust? Can our distrusts have any foundation, when we find so solid a foundation for having no distrust at all?

Do we not seem to hear this God of mercy say to each of us what He said to his cherished people of old, by the mouth of His holy prophet, Isaias: "And now thus saith the Lord, that created thee, O Jacob, and formed thee, O Israel: fear not, for I have redeemed thee, and called thee by thy name. When thou shalt pass through the waters (afflictions and tribulations) I will be with thee, and the rivers shall not cover thee: when thou shalt walk in the fire, thou shalt not be burned, and the flames shall not kindle in thee—fear not, for I am with thee, I am your Saviour;" and a little further on, he adds, "Listen, my servant, I have chosen you; I have formed thee—fear not" (Isaias xliii. 1, etc.).

What stronger motive for comfort can there be than to hear Almighty God Himself say, "fear not!" Can we hesitate to expect all from Him, Who has anticipated us, by giving us all? Happy is the man who finds in Almighty God so much mercy, and so much reason for confidence! He is still more happy in this, that not only he can trust in God with assurance, but because this God of goodness exacts this confidence, and is offended if it is refused Him, or if narrower limits are put to it than He wishes. We may also add, that not only is this confidence solid, but it is absolutely indispensable, for it is one of the most pressing duties of Christianity.

CHAPTER XIV.

NOT ONLY IS THIS CONFIDENCE ESTABLISHED ON A SOLID FOUNDATION, BUT IT APPEARS TO BE AN INDISPENSABLE OBLIGATION. THE CARE GOD TAKES TO EXCITE IT IN US.

THERE is nothing more marked in the Holy Writings than the obligation of opening our heart to this holy confidence. The whole of the Scripture appears to me to excite in us this sentiment, at once so just and so consoling. Why so many descriptions of the mercy and the infinite goodness of God Who receives, Who excuses the sinner, and Who pardons everyone who sincerely returns to Him. Why so many assurances that God loves us tenderly, that He makes it His delight to dwell among us, that He wishes to save us all, that He does not wish anyone to perish, that He orders and regulates our temptations that they might not be stronger than our ability to resist them! Why all these histories, these symbols, these touching parables?

Sometimes it is a mother who holds her infant in her arms, and who never wearies of its importunities—sometimes it is a husband who invites his faithless spouse to return to him after her wanderings, and who promises to receive her—sometimes it is a father who runs to meet and embrace his returning but prodigal son—sometimes it is an adulteress, a publican, a woman of bad life, a robber, to whom He gives the pardon of sins, and to whom He opens the gate of heaven. Why, therefore, so many instructions on His mercy, if we are at liberty to reject the consolation they offer us? and since God takes so much care to excite our confidence, is it not to oppose His designs, to remain obstinate in our distrusts, and to continue timid?

Besides, I see in the Holy Scripture, not only a law of hoping in God, but I see also that He attaches graces and rewards to that perfect hope of which I speak. It is for him who has this holy trust and confidence, that the eternal inheritance is reserved—it is he who will possess the holy mountain. "He that putteth his trust in Me, shall inherit the land, and shall possess My Holy Mount" (Isaias lvii. 13); and again, "Blessed is the man that trusteth in the Lord, and the Lord shall be his confidence. He shall be as a tree that is planted by the waters, that spreadeth out its roots towards moisture, and it shall not fear when heat cometh, and the leaf thereof shall be green, neither shall it cease at any time to bring forth fruit" (Jeremias xvii. 7); and again, in another place, "And delivering I will deliver thee.... because thou hast put thy trust in Me, saith the Lord" (Jeremias xxxix. 18).

What should still more animate the fervour of our hope, is that the Holy Spirit, in the Divine Scripture, repeats many times, even with an oath, that he who hopes is happy, that he is blessed by God, that he will never be deceived, that he will never have occasion to blush, that his confidence will never turn to his confusion. What could He do more to encourage us? It is a God Who speaks, a God Who promises, a God Who certifies, a God Who takes an oath. Does He do all this to no purpose? "Happy is the man," I will say with Tertullian, "to whom God makes so many promises, and culpable indeed is he who will not believe even the oath of his God."

To all these assurances let us add the invitations of this God of mercy, "Who loveth our souls" (Wisdom xi. 27), and Who "wishes all men to be saved" (2 Tim. ii. 4). "Come to me," said He, "come all" (St. Matt. xi. 28). The invitation is general. It is not addressed only to the Saints and to the perfect; it does not except a single individual. But are not those who are pressed down under the weight of their sins, those who have so much difficulty in overcoming their passions, and who are always fighting against temptations,—those who sigh under the weight of worldly affairs, who are engaged in occupations entirely of this earth, who are overburdened with the embarrassments caused by a family, by the possession of property, or by law-suits,—are these not excluded from the invitation of our Lord? Would they not be rejected as unworthy of being received by a God so holy and so pure?

No; these are they whom Jesus had principally in view when He calls, when He invites, when He wishes to help *all*: "Come to me," He says, "*all* you that *labour* and *are burdened*. You who endure so many combats, who meet with so much resistance; however unworthy you may be of My help, have confidence, I will assist you, I will comfort you, I will deliver you, I will give you peace and refreshment, I will crown you, I will find My glory in your salvation." For who is he that gives the most glory to God? The Prophet Baruch will answer the question: "He who is sorrowful for the greatness of his sins, and goeth bowed down and feeble, and the eyes that fail, and the hungry soul, giveth glory and justice to Thee, the Lord" (Baruch ii. 18). It is he who in his miseries returns to God, who gives Him the greatest glory by his repentance.

It is thus that God encourages us in our

weakness. Is it then in vain that He invites us to come to Him? "Would he so press us to throw ourselves into His arms," saith St. Augustine, "if He had no intention to receive us there? His promises, would they not be false and deceitful, if He excepted anyone from the super-abounding mercy which He offers us? He who hesitates whether he should throw himself into His arms, and who fears more than he hopes, does he not do an injury to Him Who has shown so much anxiety to comfort us all in our distrust?"

CHAPTER XV.

IT IS TO DO AN INJURY TO GOD TO REFUSE HIM THIS CONFIDENCE WHICH HE ASKS OF US.

IT seems, in truth, that it is to offer a sensible injury to God to abandon ourselves to these excessive fears, and to these distrusts against which I am contending; for what injury it must be to Him Who does violence to Himself, so to speak, in thus manifesting His goodness, to distrust Him still! What injustice to put limits to His mercy, which is infinite! I do not wish to authorize those who would carry this confidence even to presumption, and who take advantage of this goodness to put no limit to their transgressions. I have already said it is not for them that I write this treatise; "they shall be confounded in their expectation, and their hope is an abomination" (Job xi. 29). I speak always according to the principles I have laid down. I speak of that hope which supposes a life regulated according to the law of God, and which implies, at least, a sincere desire to begin a course of self-discipline according to this holy law. I speak only either for the just who love God, or for the repentant sinner, who wishes sincerely his own conversion, but hesitates at the view of the multitude of his sins, fearing that God will not show him mercy on their account!

With regard to the repentant sinner, I would wish that he made a scruple of his distrusts, and of his excessive fear. I tell him boldly that this distrust appears to me to be injurious to God. For, I would ask him, what makes you hesitate? Is it any question as to the power of God? but you know that His power is without any limits. How enormous soever are your iniquities, is not the mercy of God a thousand times more extended, and more abundant? Do you doubt His promises? Are not these promises of God sincere? Are they not made for you? Is it that you doubt the good-will God has for you in particular? Do you not know that He is your Father, that in consequence He loves you, that He wishes sincerely to save you, and this God, "the lover of souls," has your salvation more at heart than you have yourself? To doubt any of these truths, is it not to fail in submission to the truths which the faith teaches us, since this power of God, this fidelity to His promises, this unbounded goodness, are truths, so clearly explained and so solidly established, that we cannot call them in question; at least it is to offend the mercy of God, to set bounds to it at our own will; since this mercy is not only infinite, but the particular glory of this great attribute consists in being more "copious," according to the expression of the Royal

Prophet, than are the iniquities of the whole world, "et copiosa apud eum redemptio" (Ps. cxxix. 7).

Besides, to speak merely humanly, and according to the feeble lights of our reason, I see nothing more trying to one who has a sensitive heart, or which inflicts on him a greater injury, than to doubt his friendship, than to hesitate to believe his promises, than not to venture, through a frivolous fear, to accept his obliging offers. For the same reason, as it is an insult to a king to doubt his power, so is it injurious to a friend to doubt his tenderness and his services. Distrust, in my idea, is as injurious to friendship as ingratitude. It is itself a kind of ingratitude, when it hinders us from placing confidence in a friendship which has a thousand times been put to the proof, since we can never doubt the sincerity of a friend who offers us his services, of which in past times we cannot forget either the number or the merit. If, then, distrust and fear are so contrary to friendship, they are not the less so to charity. If they are so injurious to man, who, after all, is subject to inconstancy, are they less so to God, Who, eternal in His duration, is equally so in His mercy?

Let us complete the description of this holy confidence of which I am speaking, and after showing how solid and necessary it is, in order to make known all its advantages, we will mention some other of its characteristics. It is glorious to God, and it is an effectual means of our salvation. We find it a strength in temptation, and it animates the fervour of our charity—and it does this, by means of the spiritual joy it imparts to us. It is this holy joy which constitutes here below our most solid consolation. We will say a word on each of these advantages.

CHAPTER XVI.

OTHER CHARACTERISTICS OF CONFIDENCE IN THE MERCY OF GOD. THE FIVE ADVANTAGES WE FIND IN IT.

FIRST, this confidence is glorious to Almighty God. We are taught this by the Royal

Prophet, who had so many reasons to fear His justice, after the great sins he had committed. He felt all the shame of his sins, the sins of adultery and murder, and all the enormity of his ingratitude towards God. He wished that the justice of God should be armed against him. Yet he thought that he could not turn aside His anger more effectually than by glorifying with all his power Him whom he had blasphemed by his works.

But what homage, what praise, what glory could he give to Almighty God capable of repairing the sins he had committed? The means of doing this, in the most excellent and the most perfect manner, was, he thought, to hope in His goodness.

"I will hope in you, O Lord," he cries out, "yes I will always hope in you, and I shall crown by this homage which I render to your mercy, all the praises that man ever gave you. 'But I will always hope, and will add to all thy praise,'" (Ps. lxx. 14).

Secondly, confidence in God is a powerful help in obtaining, and in securing our salvation. The most criminal and the most corrupt sinner in the whole world, if he abandons his sins, and does penance, will find in this confidence in God, in His infinite mercy, an efficacious remedy for all his miseries. Let him afflict himself, and let him hope in God, and he shall be saved. God has said it, and He has promised it. It is for this reason, that hope is compared in the Holy Scripture to the anchor of a ship. We find this comparison made use of by St. Paul writing to the Hebrews (vi. 19). "Which hope we have as an anchor of the soul, sure and firm, and which entereth in even within the veil."

When a ship in a tempest has lost all its rigging, if the anchor remains, it will preserve it from shipwreck. It is the same with confidence in the mercy of God. We may say that it was from want of this confidence that Cain and Judas perished in their sins. Cain had irritated God by his jealousy and homicide, but what put the seal to his reprobation, was his saying in despair, " mine iniquity is greater than may deserve pardon." Judas repented of his shameful treason against our Divine Saviour. "Alas!" says St. Chrysostom, "if he had had confidence in the goodness of his Divine Master, if he had returned to Him to demand mercy, the Son of God Who pardoned the infidelity of St. Peter, and Who prayed for His murderers, would doubtless have received this traitor with mercy and forgiveness; and would have admitted him to penance."

Thirdly. This confidence is a protection, and a powerful weapon against temptations. The Holy Scripture tells us this truth in express terms—"in hope shall your strength be" (Isaias xxx. 15).

What can be stronger, than he who puts his confidence in God? To trust in God, is to repose in Him, it is to lean upon Him, it is to take for our help the attributes of God Himself, His goodness, His truth, His power. With such weapons in our hands, why, or whom should we fear, since no enemy can prevail against God. "The heart of the just," saith the Royal Prophet, "is ready to hope in the Lord, his heart is strengthened, he shall not be moved" (Ps. iii. 7).

Fourthly. It is in this confidence that we find the fervour of charity. We have already said this, when showing how fear and distrust are contrary to the love of God. We then described the difference between a distrustful and timid love, and that which the Holy Scripture demands of us, the love which "casteth out fear." Hence it is that the Prophet Isaias likens him who is animated with this virtue of confidence, to an eagle. "They that hope in the Lord shall renew their strength, they shall take wings as eagles" (Is. xl. 31).

If a fresh testimony is needed from the inspired writings, we may instance St. Paul, who, when writing to his converts, the faithful of the primitive Church in Rome, exhorts them to serve God with fervour, and also to hope in Him, as the best means of attaining that fervour. "In spirit fervent, rejoicing in hope" (Rom. xii. 12).

In truth, it is in that spiritual joy with which confidence fills the heart, that the fervour of charity principally consists—and this is the fifth characteristic of the virtue of which I am speaking—a characteristic often taken notice of in Holy Scriptures. "Thou hast given gladness in my heart," exclaims the

Royal Prophet—but how did Almighty God impart that gladness ? The Psalmist immediately after, tells us; "O Lord," he says, "thou has singularly *settled* me in hope" (Ps. iv. 10). Could we indeed help being joyous, and content, when we are assured that the most important affair we can have on earth, our salvation, is in the hands of God, Who desires it more than we do ourselves, that He thinks of it, that He labours to secure it, that He will forget nothing that may obtain for it a happy issue ? If my salvation depended on myself alone, I should be weighed down with sadness and with fear, because I know my misery, my passions, my inconstancy. But because it depends principally on God Who not only works with me, but Who goes before me, anticipating my wants, Who presses me, Who desires me to correspond with the movements of His grace, therefore it is that I am in peace, I am happy, I am in great joy, for He " has singularly *settled* me in hope." I let myself be conducted sweetly by His Providence, assured as I am, that Almighty God labours without ceasing for my happiness and my salvation. And they shall say in that day, "Lo! this is our God, we have waited for Him, we shall rejoice and be joyful in His salvation" (Isaias xxv. 9).

CHAPTER XVII.

THE SIXTH ADVANTAGE OF THIS HOLY CONFIDENCE—IT GIVES US A GREAT CONSOLATION IN OUR DIFFICULTIES AND TROUBLES.

This holy joy produces in us a solid consolation in all the events of life, and is proof against all adversities—it is the sixth characteristic of confidence in the mercy of God, and no less precious than the others. For how are we to live in this world, where all that is around us is a source of continual trouble and affliction? How, I say, are we to live in it, without consolation? yet where are we to find what is so necessary for us? For it is not to be found in the society in which we live, nor in the possession of property, nor in the enjoyment of pleasure, all this is too limited, too feeble, too inconstant, to procure us solid happiness, or true joy.

If we find in what is created, any consolation, it is only a consolation in passing, which amuses the heart, but cannot fill it. How many troubles are there, in which neither property, nor pleasure, nor friends, can bring us any solid comfort! But we find the comfort we want in confidence in God, and in His love. What true consolation there is in being loved by God! in being the object of His caresses, and of His complacency! What consolation to think that He is preparing for us a crown, with which all that the earth has of beauty and of glory is not to be compared! What consolation to call to mind, and to be sure, that He is conducting us to it by all the events of life, whether pleasurable or painful, and that those which appear the most sad, and the most afflicting, are the most effectual means He could employ to succeed in His design!

What consolation, in the midst of harassing temptations, to know that if Almighty God permits the demon to attack us, He only gives him this power in *measure*, and in proportion to our strength, and that where that strength seems to fail us, this "faithful God," as St. Paul says, " will not suffer us to be tried above our strength, but will with the temptation make issue, that we may be able to bear it" (1 Cor. x. 13).

What consolation at the remembrance of all our past sins, when we are tempted to despair, and at the discouraging sight of our daily imperfections—what consolation, I say, to think that all this has not wearied the patience of our God, that His infinite mercy is greater than all our iniquities, and that in the moment when we love Him with all our heart, and that we trust in His goodness, this infinite mercy receives us with tenderness, and in His love wishes to blot out for ever what might excite His anger, or produce in ourselves excessive fear. What consolation, even when we are in the greatest trial, when all is darkness and obscurity, when we see in ourselves hardly anything but sin, and in God only His anger, when we dare not say to ourselves that we love God, and when it seems almost that we cease to hope or to believe in Him, so violent are our temptations—what consolation, I say, to think that God is so merciful and good, that with Him, to *wish* to serve Him is counted as a service, and to *wish* to love is counted as love—what consolation to remember that He reckons our desires in the number of our merits, and will crown them as He crowns our victories! Oh! you who are timid and distrustful, open your hearts to this consolation. "You that fear the Lord, wait for His mercy, and go not aside from Him lest you fall. You that fear the Lord, believe in Him, and your reward shall not be made void. You that fear the Lord, hope in Him, and mercy shall come to you for your delight" (Ecclesiast. ii. 7, 8, 9).

Such is the consolation we may find in all the conditions of life, even the most afflicting. This consolation is real, it is solid, it does not depend on events, nor on creatures. The perfidy of friends, the misfortunes of life, the loss of property, cannot deprive us of it; on the contrary, it increases in proportion as our misfortunes become more bitter, since the most certain assurance that we can have of the help of God is when we are abandoned by all other help that is human and earthly. Now, where can we find this consolation? It is only in confidence in God. It is this confidence which opens to us all the consoling truths I have just mentioned—it is confidence in God which makes us feel all their sweetness. Without it, alas! how can we keep ourselves from discouragement and despair? What I have said, then, may suffice to unfold to us the advantages and the characteristics of confidence in God, its sweetness, its joy, its consolation, its necessity, and the solid foundations on which it is supported. To render this instruction complete, it only remains for me to examine into the motives of that fear which alarms so many souls, to disabuse them of the reason of their distrust, and to reply to all the objections and difficulties urged against those sentiments of confidence with which I would endeavour to inspire them. This I propose doing in the second part of this work.

SECOND PART.

IN WHICH THE OBJECTIONS SUGGESTED TO THE TIMID BY FEAR ARE ANSWERED.

CHAPTER I.

OBJECTIONS OF THE TIMID AND SCRUPULOUS. FIRST OBJECTION, THE STRICT AND SEVERE JUSTICE OF GOD. DESCRIPTION OF THE SEVERITY OF HIS JUDGMENTS.

IT is in what the Faith teaches us of the severity of God's judgments, and of the rigours of His justice, that the timid find the first source of their fear. In truth, I allow it, there is much in this severity to affright us, and it is impossible, in reading the description the Holy Scriptures give us of the divine judgments, for the holiest, and even the most presumptuous, not to feel terror. Sometimes it is a Holy God, Who is irritated with the slightest stains; sometimes it is a jealous God, Who is offended by the least division of affection; sometimes it is a God taking vengeance, Who makes the whole earth suffer the punishment of a crime committed by a few only of its inhabitants, and, in His indignation, makes His chastisements to fall even on the fourth generation, in expiation of a crime committed in years that have long passed away.

What we learn from the Holy Scriptures of His character as a judge, and of the exactitude and the rigour of His judgments, is not less terrible; for with what exactness will He not hereafter enter into the discussion of all our actions, and not only of our actions, but of our words and our desires, and even of our most secret and indifferent thoughts! What may escape our attention will not escape His investigation; all will be discussed; a word which has nothing in it criminal will have to be accounted for, because it was an "idle word;" an injurious word which has escaped us in anger, will be punished; a feeling of concupiscence, which escapes our notice, and passes off without reflection, will have to bear its penalty.

Not only is Almighty God irritated with the evil we have done, but He imputes to us sometimes the evil we have not done, and of which we knew nothing; it is sufficient that we have either procured it, or that we have permitted it, or even sometimes that we have suffered it in silence. This silence is often criminal in His sight—another proof of the exactitude of this severe judge. It is not only the sinner on whom He pronounces this censure. If the just is not just *enough*, if he is tepid in his love, if he is slothful in the duties of penance, if he does not correspond by good works to the graces he has received, if, in doing works of holiness, he does not do them holily, and, as the Scripture saith, "If his works are not full before Him, this just man should fear His severity. For I find not thy works full before my God" (Apocal. iii. 2).

Such are the judgments of our God; judgments terrible by the examination we shall have to pass, but no less terrible by the surprise with which He may overtake us by these judgments; for when is it that this God, so avenging and so severe, will come to pass His judgments upon us? We do not know. He hides His coming, He has said, and He executes it to the letter. "It will be at an hour when you think not" (St. Luke xii. 40), and when we think ourselves safe, for He will come "as a thief in the night" (1 Thess. v. 2). He conceals His approach, and He will take us by surprise. In fact, He often now surprises the sinner without giving him the leisure to do penance.

He surprises him in the midst of his business, in the midst of his pleasures, in the midst even of his sins. He summons him away, to render Him an account, and what appears still more terrifying, He passes judgment on those who resist Him during this life, without waiting for the last moment. He lays His hand upon them to afflict them, or He withdraws His mercy from them, and thus lets them fall, like Pharaoh of old, into hardness of heart; He deprives them of that help which they render useless, and the time comes when the sinner calls on Him in vain, when he seeks Him, but does not find Him, when he invokes Him, and this irritated God does not listen to him, because he has left him; He hides Himself from him, and will not show Himself to him any more, till the terrible moment of his impenitent death; when, to quote the awful words of the Holy Scripture, "He will laugh in his destruction, and will mock when that shall come upon him which he feared" (Prov. i. 26). That no one may think that I exaggerate this description of the judgments of God, I may remark, that all these truths, and almost all my expressions, are the truths and the expressions which we find in the Holy Scripture itself.

Who is there, then, who will not understand that God is a God terrible in His vengeance, and that nothing is more terrifying than His judgments? Who will not cry out with the Royal Prophet, who was terrified at them even to fainting: "How terrible are Thy judgments, O Lord?" "The sins of my youth and my ignorances do not remember" (Ps. xxiv. 7). "For if Thou, O Lord, wilt mark iniquities, Lord, who shall stand?" (Ps. cxxix. 3).

It is this, then, that affrights both the just and the timid penitent—the severity of God's judgments. But let us see if there is not a remedy for this impression of terror, which these truths produce in the soul.

CHAPTER II.

REPLY TO THE FIRST OBJECTION. HOW TERRIBLE SOEVER GOD IS, HE IS STILL MORE AMIABLE. WHAT ADVANTAGE IT IS FOR US TO HAVE JESUS CHRIST FOR OUR JUDGE.

IT is true that God is judge, that He is our judge, and that under this title of judge He is severe. But is He a judge that will not be appeased, Who may not be gained, Who will not pardon? He takes the sinner by surprise, He examines, He punishes—but at the same time, I see He gives notice that He threatens—that He waits, that He receives, that He pardons, that He loves, that He compassionates, that He is appeased—that it is as easy to move Him to mercy during this life, as it is impossible to pacify Him at the judgment after death; I see that He takes the character of a judge, of a judge strong and mighty, but that the Holy Scripture adds also the qualities of justice, and patience, and goodness. "God is a just judge, strong and patient" (Ps. xii. 7). Would I have more to give me encouragement.

I see Him, in the Gospel, under the figure of a father of a family, who is irritated with the infidelities of his steward, and who says to him in his anger, "Render an account of thy stewardship." Would you not think he was going to punish him? No! this steward, made rich by presents, even at the expense of his master (the symbol of alms that a sinner gives out of the property he has received from God, to appease Him at his conversion, for this is the true sense of the parable), this father of a family, I say, ceased to be irritated against him, though he had so much reason to be so.

He is appeased, he praises, he applauds the address and ability of his steward, of whom he had such reason to complain. I see Him again under the figure of a powerful king, to whom many millions are due by a miserable debtor, whom the king cites before him, questions, and reproaches for his negligence. The debtor humbles himself, and asks for time. Not only this merciful king grants him what he asks, but he forgives him all the debt he owes.

Again, I see Him under the figure of another father of a family, who goes to seek labourers to work in his vineyard. He finds some idle, who passed the day without doing anything; he reproaches them for their idleness, and, it seems, with indignation. These people are touched with his warnings: they work one hour. But what can workmen do in one hour? They had nothing to be commended for while at their work, but their good-will. It is this good-will that the father of the family rewards with the same liberality as if they had worked all the day!

Once more, I see Him in the prophet who complains of the wanderings of his people, and reproaches them for it. It is a God and a judge Who speaks, but it is not the language of a God nor of a judge. When He speaks as

God He thunders, He strikes with the bolts of His anger, He punishes. "He uttered His voice, the earth trembled," saith the Royal Prophet (Ps. xlv. 7). A judge does not utter a complaint, he pronounces a just and irreversible sentence. He condemns, he punishes. It is love which complains—a father, a brother, a friend complains, and whilst he complains he manifests still his friendship. It is thus that God complains, when he would punish. It is love which makes Him utter these complaints, and we must not misunderstand Him —He complains, and to whom?

To the one himself, of whom He complains, and He does this to touch and move him—and without harshness or bitterness. When we complain of our friend, to himself, and we do this with sweetness, is it not a mark that we are ready to receive his excuses, and to forgive him without difficulty? Oh, how favourable is a judge when he loves thus, and still more when he desires to be loved. Such is our God. Can we, after this, allow our fear to trouble and to cast us down? It is for the hardened, for the presumptuous, for the impenitent to tremble at the remembrance of His anger. But for those who wish to serve Him, if they ought to fear, it seems to me that they ought still more to love Him.

Observe also that if Almighty God is our Judge, we must bear in mind that He is also our Father, our Spouse, our Friend, our Brother, our Advocate and our Saviour. How many consoling titles, for a single one that is terrifying. Is not the single one which is so fearful, to be counterbalanced by those other qualities which are so amiable? Seeing the many different shapes which His mercy takes to save us, for the only one by which He manifests His justice, have we not reason to comfort ourselves in our alarms, and to say, with the Royal Prophet, that "His tender mercies, especially in regard to us, are over all His works, all the works of His power" (Ps. cxliv. 9)?

Let us add here the beautiful thought of St. Chrysostom. He is explaining that prayer of the Royal Prophet, in which he asks of God to give His judgments and His justice to His Son. "Give to the King thy judgments, O

God, and to the King's Son Thy justice" (Ps. lxxi. 1).

Wherefore, says this Father, does the Prophet demand that God would despoil Himself of His power, to clothe with it His Son made man? Why has God, graciously hearing this prayer of His servant, in truth, committed to Jesus Christ the power to judge the living and the dead, as He Himself assures us in the holy Gospel? Is it that judgment in the hands of God the Father had not been exercised with sufficient justice? No! without doubt His judgments have been always equitable—but they had been also terrible. Were a holy God to judge sinners, were a God incapable of passions to judge men subject to passions, were a God mighty and irritated to judge men feeble and culpable, alas! there would be nothing but chastisement for them to expect. But that they should be judged by a man like themselves, who has experienced their miseries, and carried their sins, who became, by taking the same nature, their Brother, their Friend, and their Saviour, then, instead of having everything to fear and little to hope for, they have on the contrary very much more to hope for than they have to fear. This Judge which they have obtained has every disposition to be favourable in their regard.

It is, then, for this reason, says St. Chrysostom, that the Royal Prophet desired that judgment should be remitted into the hands of the King's Son. It is for our consolation that God, by an effect of His mercy, has been willing to strip Himself, so to speak, of this title of Judge, to clothe with it His Son. But this is not all we have to comfort us. I add further, that in Jesus Christ, this title even of Judge, which, after all, might appear terrible, is well fitted to calm us in our distrusts. It is one of the most consoling titles of the Son of God.

CHAPTER III.

CONTINUATION OF THE SAME SUBJECT. JESUS CHRIST IS THE MOST FAVOURABLE OF ALL JUDGES. FIRST, BECAUSE HE IS FULL OF GOODNESS, AND KINDNESS.

As we must all be judged, could we find in the whole world a judge in whom we could place greater hope and confidence than in the Son of God? I can see none, either in heaven, or on earth, who could be more disposed to show us favour. In truth, if God had given me the liberty of choosing for myself a judge who should decide my eternity, that judge would not be my father, nor my brother, nor my friend; it would be Jesus Christ, Whom I should wish to take upon Himself the office of my Judge. For however favourable might be the dispositions of any other, do I not find them much more so in my Saviour? First I should desire in my Judge, that he should be full of an unexampled goodness and kindness; in the second place, that he knew perfectly every circumstance that might serve me as an excuse, and that he knew it, if that were possible, of himself, and by his own experience. I should wish also that he had a true love for me, that he was my own friend, my intimate friend. I should wish that this friend, besides his friendship for me, should have a personal interest in passing a favourable judgment, and in saving me. This is the judge I should like to have, and that every one else would wish to have, as well as myself. If we seek among men for all these qualities, we shall not find them in any one else but in Jesus Christ. I see them in Him in a degree which far surpasses what I might meet with among men.

As to goodness, can we find any one to be compared with Him? Recall to mind what we have already said of his incomprehensible goodness. Who is there on earth whose goodness is to be compared with His? for His goodness is as infinite as His power, as His Eternity, and all His other perfections. Remember also what has been said of His tenderness for us. He is afflicted, He sighs, He weeps for us. He is more touched with our miseries than we are ourselves. If we would have a fresh proof of this, we have only to consider the different states of life in which we find Him while on earth, and the figures under which He is represented in the New Testament. To give us more easy access to Him, He became a little infant. He became a man, to share with us our miseries. He is made a slave, to set us at liberty; poor, that we may be made rich; and victim, for our purification. He takes the title of Father, that we may become His children; that of Master, that we may hear His voice; that of Spouse, to excite our tenderness; that of Mediator and surety, in order to deliver us; that of King, that we may submit ourselves to Him. He is the way, which conducts us by a sure road; the truth, which instructs us by solid maxims; the life, which animates us, in order to make us happy and immortal. If we are sinners He is our justice; if in darkness, He is our light; if we are in affliction, He is our patience; if we are weak, He is our strength; if we fear death, He is the resurrection and the life; and if we wish to be happy, He is Himself our felicity.

Do we need other proofs of His goodness?

See His pressing anxiety to lead us back from our wanderings. Imagine Him, such as the Holy Gospel portrays Him, sometimes standing at the door of our heart to watch for the moment when He will be able to enter: " Behold, I stand at the door and knock" (Apoc. iii. 20). Sometimes fatigued with the long delays of our ingratitude, and sitting down in sadness to await us:—" Jesus, therefore, being wearied with His journey, sat thus on the well" (St. John iv. 6). Sometimes raising His plaintive voice with tears to soften our hardness:—"And when He drew near to Jerusalem, He wept over it" (St. Luke xix. 41). Figure to yourself this charitable Pastor exhausting His strength in seeking the lost sheep. According to justice it was for this sheep to seek the Shepherd. But His goodness does not allow Him to await its return. He follows it, He seeks it, and when He has found it, instead of being irritated against it, and giving it blows, He lays it upon His shoulder, not to hinder it from running away, but to relieve its weariness; He knows that it is fatigued with its wanderings, He fears it will be wearied out before it reaches the fold, and He forgets how fatigued He is Himself with seeking it. In this parable we have an image, a feeble image, of the goodness of Jesus in our regard. Can we doubt that He is good, that He is very good, that He is infinitely good, that He is good even to excess, if there could be any excess in His goodness? Could we find on earth any judge who had so much?

CHAPTER IV.

SECONDLY. JESUS CHRIST IS A JUDGE FULL OF COMPASSION.

A PART of His goodness consists in compassionating our weaknesses. It is another quality that we would desire in our judge, and that we find in Jesus Christ. He compassionates us as God, because as God he has created us, and therefore "He knoweth our frame," and "remembereth that we are dust" (Ps. cii. 13, 14). He knows the miseries of our feeble nature. Much more, then, will He compassionate us as man, because it is as man that He had willed to experience them Himself, even to being tempted by the devil. With the exception of the suffering of sin, our Lord had every other kind of suffering. "For we have not a high priest," saith St. Paul, "who cannot have compassion on our infirmities, but was tempted in all things like as we are, without sin" (Heb. iv. 13). In fact, though He was God, His human soul, in the midst of His temptations, was "sorrowful even unto death." He was prostrated to the earth at the view of the trials through which he was to pass, and His Body suffered in consequence a sweat of blood. He prayed to His Heavenly Father in the garden, that the chalice of suffering whose bitterness terrified Him, might pass from Him. It is true that these movements of fear and of sadness were the effect of His own Will, in the inferior part of His soul, and that He felt them only because He willed them. But after all, He did feel them, and it is enough to make Him compassionate those in whom these sentiments and these feelings are involuntary. It is enough that He does not exact from them an impossible insensibility, impossible to our nature, and that He pardons more easily those who cry to Him from the depth of their misery and their weakness, of which He knows by His own experience all the weight. Thus the Church asks of Him mercy, by His sadness, by His weakness, by His agony, and by His temptation. In fact, it is by these miseries, of which, in His goodness, He deigned to partake (in order to experience them as we do), that He seems more inclined to compassionate those which are, in ourselves, the source of so many sins.

CHAPTER V.

THIRDLY. JESUS CHRIST IS AT THE SAME TIME OUR JUDGE AND OUR FRIEND.

Our Judge is full of goodness, and He is as compassionate as good. I add, in the third place, that He is our best, our most intimate, our most tender friend, for this is the title He has condescended to give us, and to take Himself in our regard. "You are my friends," He said to His Apostles; and again: "I call you not servants, but friends." Jesus, then, takes in our regard the name and title of friend; it is another reason for hoping of Him a favourable judgment. For on whatever friend you count, you will find there are still more and stronger reasons for counting on the friendship of Jesus Christ. Your friend loves you tenderly, he has told you so a thousand times; he is ready to serve you on every occasion, and he has given you many proofs of it. This is a great love; but however great it is, can it be compared with that of Jesus Christ? Your friend has only his heart to give you, and this heart is small, is very little, it is but the heart of a man. But the Heart of Jesus is, indeed, great; it is immense, it is infinite, it is the Heart of God. The friendship of your friend is weak and incapable; on how many occasions he is only able to help you by his tears; that of Jesus Christ is strong and mighty—nature, hell, and death are subject to His Will; the love of your friend is but recent, it commenced only a few years since, when he first made your acquaintance; that of Jesus Christ is much more ancient, it dates from eternity. Before all time He had for you thoughts of mercy and salvation; it was eighteen centuries ago that He prepared for you, by the shedding of His Precious Blood, the means of enriching you for ever. The friendship of your friend is, perhaps, an interested one—he hopes for your protection and assistance, or, at least, it is the pleasure he finds in your society that attaches him to you; that of Jesus has no other interest than your own. He is rich, He is happy, He is glorious, He is God without you, and He loves you only for your own good, and in order to make you infinitely happy. Your friend's friendship is frail and uncertain; an offence, a jealousy, a hasty reply,—less than that, a forgetfulness, a slight, an unconscious want of respect or of attention, cools sometimes the most tender attachments; that of Jesus is constant and durable: a thousand and a thousand offences have not yet discouraged Him; and though you have despised His voice for a long time back, and perhaps actually despise it still, while you are reading these lines, yet He speaks to you, He presses you, He says to you tenderly, "My son, give

Me your heart, as I have given you Mine" (Prov. xxiii. 26).

I will say more: your friend, your brother, your husband, he that loves you the most tenderly, have they ever given their life for you? Jesus has done this. Have they ever pardoned your sins and your many acts of ingratitude? Jesus has done this. Have they ever become poor, that you might be rich? Jesus has done this. Will they ever place you upon a throne? Jesus will do this. Will they ever make you eternally happy? Jesus has spared nothing to procure you this eternal happiness. Judge, then, after this, if His friendship is not to be preferred to that of any other. To which of these two friends will you now give your confidence? Will it be to this man, or to Jesus? Which of these two friendships is capable of giving you comfort? Is there any one who does not feel that it is to Jesus Christ and to His friendship that he ought to give the preference? Should we not, then, be ashamed, after this, to fear His judgment, to prefer the judgment of a man, whose friendship is to be despised, in comparison with that of Jesus

Christ? Yes, it is He, since He permits me to call Him so, Who is truly my friend and the friend of my heart. What do I say? Not only my Friend, but also my Brother, my Spouse, my Deliverer, and my Father; uniting in Himself all these titles, He unites in Himself all those sentiments of tenderness which it is in the nature of these titles to inspire. In multiplying the titles of His affection, He multiplies also, so to speak, the claims I hope to have on His mercy.

CHAPTER VI.

FOURTHLY.   JESUS CHRIST IS A JUDGE WHO IS INTERESTED IN OUR SALVATION.

IN these titles, then, I find a fresh reason for placing my confidence in the judgment of Jesus Christ, because they move Him to judge me with mercy. I have said, that in the choice of a judge, we should wish to have one interested in our favour. It is Jesus Christ Who is this Judge, it is His interest in every way to save us. Interest of His glory:—He finds it in gaining my heart, in spite of my rebellions. He finds it in forgetting my sins, in spite of my unworthiness—the greater sinner I am, the more He displays the magnificence of His mercies. It is thus, that He triumphs in His Saints. In them he is glorious. He is glorified in the sight of the whole universe, which sees that He is God in His mercy, as He is God in His justice. Interest, so to speak, of His riches:—would He be content to lose all the riches which He expended in my regard? I have cost him so much to redeem me—would He lose without necessity and without fruit the price of my salvation? Interest, too, of parentage and family, since He calls us His Brothers, His Children, His Spouses. Does not a father interest himself about the salvation of his own children? a husband, about the salvation of his own wife? a brother, of his brother? It is by these titles, that Jesus Christ loves us—it is also by these titles that He will interest Himself to save us. Such is the thought of the author of Ecclesiasticus where he says,

"The compassion of man is towards his neighbour, but the mercy of God is upon all flesh" (Ecclesiast. xviii. 12); that is to say, that the love of sinners is shown more particularly to their family, but that God, who counts all mankind in His family, has for all mankind as much mercy and love as we have for those who are allied to us by the ties of blood.

I will add further, that Jesus Christ feels and takes greater interest in our salvation, than we feel and take in it ourselves.

If a pagan has said (Juvenal) "that man is dearer to the Gods than he is to himself," with much more reason may we say that we are more dear to Jesus Christ than we are to ourselves. The proof is, that he has done more for our salvation than we do for it ourselves. What has He not done, and what is He not doing for it still? We—alas! what are *we* doing for our salvation? I find the zeal of Jesus Christ, and His ardent desire to save us, portrayed in the Gospel parables in a striking manner. I see them figured in the parable of the woman who seeks with diligence for the piece of money she had lost; in that of the good shepherd, who goes after the sheep that had wandered from the fold. After much labour and care they both find what they sought, and immediately they assemble their friends, to tell them the good news, as we ourselves are wont to do. They bring together their friends, that they may be congratulated on their success—and observe that the good shepherd does not say, congratulate my sheep for his happy and safe return, that it has escaped the teeth of ferocious beasts—no—it is himself who wishes to be congratulated. Rejoice with me, because I am full of joy. I am so transported with it, that I seek some one to share it with me. All the difficulties and dangers through which I have passed are nothing to me now. Would you not say that the happiness and the wealth of this good shepherd were centred in this one sheep, and that without it, he would be neither rich nor happy? It is thus, O my Saviour, that You seek us, and that You interest Yourself in our salvation. Unhappy is he who is not touched with these solicitudes of our Divine Redeemer. Unhappy is he who does not find in this unexampled goodness, wherewith to comfort himself in his distrust.

But the timid and distrustful will reply, Jesus Christ is indeed our Friend, our Father, He is compassionate, He is interested in our salvation, but after all He is just. May He not be irritated against me, who am a sinner? What will prevent Him from passing a terrible sentence against me? for I deserve His chastisements. It is in vain you describe the titles of His mercy, you must always acknowledge the claims of justice. Yes! it is true, we must always acknowledge them. But, I add, this is no reason why we should indulge in excessive fear. In order to convince the timid of this, I further assert, that it is this very justice which should be the principal ground of their hope. Yes! we have more to hope from God, because He is just, than we should have, if he were not just. This great truth I shall explain in the next chapter.

CHAPTER VII.

FIFTHLY. GOD IS A JUDGE INFINITELY JUST; IT IS PRECISELY BECAUSE HE IS SO JUST THAT WE OUGHT TO HOPE IN HIM.

IN order to understand what I have just said, we must call to mind that the penitent sinner does not ask for mercy of his God, but in virtue of an incontestible right he has to obtain it. What is this right? it is that which comes from Jesus Christ; it is that which comes to us through His infinite merits. If the sinner demanded mercy in his own name, if he asked for it through the virtue of his own tears, if he asked for it through the merit of his own good works, his prayer would be slighted, and unworthy to be heard. But what price does he offer to purchase this mercy? it is the satisfaction of the Son of God; His blessed Passion, His Cross, His Blood, His Tears, His Wounds, His Death, a price equal in value to the mercy of God, and worthy of all the graces he may expect through it, however infinite these graces may be, and however unworthy the sinner may be of them. The Royal Prophet, astonished at the justice of God, cried out in his fear and wonder, "if Thou, O Lord, wilt mark iniquities, Lord, who shall stand it?"—who shall be able to stand the severity of Thy just judgments? but immediately he adds, to give himself and us the greatest consolation, "for with Thee there is merciful forgiveness"—and why?—"by reason of Thy law, I have waited for Thee, O Lord, because with the Lord there is mercy, and with Him plentiful (copiosa) redemption." Because there is in Him an abundant and most copious redemption; "and He shall redeem Israel from all his iniquities, however numerous they may have been" (Ps. cxxix.).

It is then by means of this plentiful redemption, that we can satisfy all the claims of the justice of God. We find this treasure in Jesus Christ, in Whom is our treasure also; through Him we present it to His Father—and we have a right, with such a sum in our hands, to obtain what we ask for, and to expect everything we want from His infinite mercy. It is this thought which consoles me when I stand at the altar, and have the honour and inestimable privilege to hold in my hands the precious Body of my Saviour, and His priceless Blood. I think I have then a right to say, "my Father and my God! if you are irritated against me, behold with what I satisfy you. This treasure which I hold is mine, because Jesus Christ has given it to me. But this treasure is of infinite value, and as infinite as are your graces, and your mercy. Put the salvation I hope for, and the paradise I ask of you, put all your benefits and blessings at as high a price as you will, behold their equivalent in value, behold this precious Blood is enough to satisfy you for all my sins, to appease your justice, and to obtain for my soul and body everlasting life."

The sinner does not, then, say, "look on *me* O Lord,"—on the contrary, confused at the misery he sees in himself, he says what St. Peter said in his consternation, "depart from me, for I am a sinful man, O Lord" (Luke v. 8).

He casts his eyes on the ground, because he does not dare to lift them up towards heaven, for fear, it would seem, of attracting the look of God, or like Mary Magdalen, who washed with her tears the feet of Jesus Christ, placing herself behind Him (Luke vii. 38).

But if the sinner does not dare to show himself, he says, "Lord, look on Thy Son" (Ps. lxxxiii. 10). Behold His wounds, and His blood, and you will be appeased. What am I saying? is it the sinner who speaks? No! it is the Son of God Himself, Who asks His Father for the sinner, and clothing Himself, so to speak, in the person of the sinner, says for him and in his name, "my Father, I have sinned;" at the same time, He offers to His irritated Father the infinite treasures of His merits to satisfy all the demands of His justice, and thereby this justice becomes itself favourable to us.

It is in this sense that Jesus Christ is not only our Mediator, but He is also, saith St. John, our advocate with the Father. "If any man sin, we have an advocate with the Father, Jesus Christ the Just" (1 St. John ii. 2). There is a difference between these two titles. A mediator demands mercy; he demands it, even when it is not merited; he demands it, but with a sort of fear; but the advocate demands *justice;* he demands it with firmness, he demands it with authority, and with assurance. If the tribunal before which he pleads is a just and enlightened one, he demands it in virtue of the documents which he produces. Far from being alarmed at the justice of that tribunal, it is in its justice that he places his confidence. It is thus that Jesus Christ pleads for us; it is thus that He speaks with authority and with confidence. He speaks with His titles in His hands, and His titles are as incontestable as His wounds are manifest and visible. He preserves their scars even in heaven, in order to show them without ceasing to His Father as the price of His mercies. What have we to fear, then, at the tribunal of God, when such an Advocate undertakes our defence? However severe this tribunal may be, after all, it is just, and since it is just, what can it refuse to Jesus Christ? The more just it is, the more reason we have to expect a favourable sentence.

CHAPTER VIII.

CONTINUATION OF THE SAME THOUGHT. ANOTHER REASON PROVES THAT EVEN THE JUSTICE OF GOD OUGHT TO STRENGTHEN OUR CONFIDENCE.

LET us add a second reason. There is nothing more fit to remove the fears of the faithful than to show them that even the justice of God interests itself in our salvation. I draw this reason from the promises that God has made us. I dare to say it, I think Almighty God is obliged, even by His justice, to give us whatever He has promised us in His mercy. In truth, is there anything more just than to keep His word, than to be faithful to His promise? Many and many times He has promised us pardon whenever we return to Him with a contrite and humble heart. It is true that it is through His great mercy that He has engaged thus to receive us, but as He has condescended to engage His word, this God (Whom St. Paul calls a God faithful to His promise), will, by fidelity to His justice, execute and fulfil the promises which, in the tenderness of

His mercy, He has made us. Observe what extent He gives to this promise: "In what day soever he shall turn from his wickedness, the wickedness of the wicked shall not hurt him" (Ezek. xxiii. 12). And again: "If the wicked do penance for all his sins .... living he shall live, and not die" (Ezek. xviii. 21). He does not address these words to the feeble, or to those who are led astray by human frailty, but even to the wicked. This word comprehends all that is most odious and displeasing to God;—the sacrilegious, atheists, blasphemers, idolaters, and the profane, all of whom will receive mercy if they ask for it with the proper disposition. He does not say if they seek His mercy a long time, if they merit it, if they purchase it by their own good works; no, He lays down no other condition but the sincerity and uprightness of the heart that makes the demand. He will receive it, not after long solicitations, but on the very day of the demand. The same sun which shall see the penance of the sinner, shall see also his pardon, God wishing to practise Himself what He enjoins upon us in the Holy Scriptures:

"Let not the sun go down on your anger" (Eph. iv. 26), provided, that is, that the sinner does not sleep in his sin. Behold, then, what is promised—what I demand of God—and, I am bold to say, that I have a claim upon Him for it, in virtue of His promises, and in the Name and through the merits of Jesus Christ.

It is true, that in promising pardon to him who does penance, who turns to Him with a truly penitent and contrite heart, God has not promised to forgive him who defers his conversion; if the sinner puts off his repentance till the next day, he puts himself in danger of being lost. It is this which prevents him from drawing any unjust consequences from these merciful promises. He has no warrant from them to delay his conversion even for a single hour. God has not promised to await the end of these delays; on the contrary, the same Scripture which promises him pardon, assures him of the surprise of a sudden death, which may deprive him of the opportunity of demanding pardon. But as that which consoles the true penitent ought not to warrant the impenitent sinner, so what alarms the sinner ought not to trouble the penitent. The penitent ought to believe that God graciously hears his prayers, since, as I have said, it is not only the character of His mercy to do so, but an obligation of His justice as well. St. Paul was convinced of this when he said, "There is laid up for me a crown of justice, which the Lord, the just judge, will render me in that day, and not only to me, but to them also that love His coming" (2 Tim. iv. 8), words which appear bold, but which are true in their full extent, particularly according to the sense in which I have explained the word justice as applied to God. It was not on the labours of the apostolate, nor on his own good works, that the apostle founded this title of justice.

We see clearly that he gives the same right to all those who desired the coming of God's kingdom. He knew well that it is not in our good works that we can put our confidence. For as saith St. Augustine, "woe to the life the most holy, if God examines it without mercy." It is this (I say it in passing) which consoles the penitent, who is afflicted because he has not good works to offer, and who draws from it a reason for discouragement. It is not so much your good works which God demands as a condition of your forgiveness, it is the conversion of your heart, it is the love of your heart, it is the confidence of your heart—with that, you have every ground for hope. But let us return to the Apostle—in what then did he found this reward of a crown of justice which he so confidently expected. Without doubt, it was founded on the promises of God, and on the merits of Jesus Christ. Let us acknowledge it to the glory of our God, and for the consolation of those whom fear has thrown into discouragement and dejection, that notwithstanding the severity of the eternal judgments, the just man and the penitent sinner find, both the one and the other, in the justice of God wherewith to nourish and excite their confidence. If the justice even of this severe tribunal favours us, how much more favourable will be the decision, if we add to that justice of God, all that we may hope for, from His mercy. What more solid confidence can we have, than that which reposes at once both on justice and on mercy? Since then justice also sustains our confidence, ought we not to find in it our consolation, and to say with the Royal Prophet, "I remembered, O Lord, Thy judgments of old, and I was comforted?" (Ps. cxix. 52).

CHAPTER IX.

SECOND OBJECTION OF THE TIMOROUS; THE GREATNESS AND THE MULTITUDE OF THEIR SINS.

WE have now considered the first objection urged by the over timid, and we have drawn from the objection itself, a ground of hope and consolation. But this is not enough for them. The justice of God is not that which makes them anxious—it is their sins; they see their multitude and their enormity, and they hardly dare to hope for forgiveness. This is the second obstacle to their having the confidence with which I would inspire them—an obstacle which we must remove by additional reflexions.

It is true that our sins are great, and our

ingratitude also; that our infidelities are frequent, and that they do not merit in themselves any mercy. It is true that there is much to be afraid of, not only for those who stagnate in the disorders of a life wholly worldly, but also for the half-devout who allow themselves to fall, without scruple, into what they call slight faults, multiplying daily and voluntarily their infidelities to a countless number. Such cannot be too much alarmed at the just severities of Almighty God. For when they do not fear to sin they cannot too much fear the justice of Him who always punishes sin, sooner or later.

But it is not for these relaxed and presumptuous persons that I am writing. I have said it many times, and I shall never tire of repeating it, that I wish by this Treatise, to strengthen the weak, and not to encourage the presumptuous. It is then for those who are weak and timorous, that I write, for those who fear to sin, and who wish to abandon, and to renounce it for ever; it is for those who love God truly, sincerely, and cordially, at least, who wish thus to love Him; it is, in fine, for those who, not thinking that they love Him enough, are troubled in consequence, and sorrow bitterly—for this is to love always, and to love truly. It is to such that I say with Jesus Christ, "Have confidence, your sins are forgiven you; however great, however enormous, however numerous they are, the mercy of God is still more abundant." This mercy is only for the miserable, as redemption is only for captives, and pardon only for sinners. It is then for sinners, for captives, for the miserable, to hope in God's infinite mercy. The more wretched and miserable they are, and the greater are their sins, so much the more they ought to hope in the mercy of God. Let us show this truth more clearly, and teach the faithful to form a just idea of the extent of the mercy of our God. If God hated the sinner as long as the sinner was living upon this earth; if He forgot him, so long as He was forgotten by him; if instead of waiting for him with patience, He visited his sin in anger, without delay; if He rejected him, when he returned to Him; if He was inexorable when the sinner demanded pardon with humility—alas, there would be then a motive for giving way to fear.

Despair even, might then seem reasonable. But it is not with such characteristics that I recognize my God and my Saviour. I see on the contrary, that He loves the sinner; that far from forgetting, He recalls him without ceasing from his wanderings; that instead of being wearied out with his delays, He waits for Him with eagerness; that He forgives him easily, and receives him with tenderness, on his return. Such is the portrait the Scripture gives us of the mercy and the goodness of our God. Let us consider all these characteristics in detail.

CHAPTER X.

REPLY TO THE FOREGOING OBJECTION. THE SENTIMENTS OF GOD TOWARDS THE SINNER ARE THE SENTIMENTS OF MERCY; HE LOVES HIM, AND IS MOVED WITH TENDERNESS TOWARDS HIM, IN THAT HE IS A SINNER.

GOD hates sin, I allow, but He never wearies of loving the sinner. He loves him with tenderness. It seems that it is sufficient to be a sinner to share in this tenderness of His love. And why should He not love him? Sinner as he is, he is still His creature, and His own work, and, what is more, he is His child. It is this which is represented to us in figure, by the tenderness of that holy king, who, driven from his throne by an unnatural son, yet continued to have for him all the tenderness of a father, though to ensure his own safety he was compelled to take arms against him, and to treat him as a rebel. The sin of Absalom could not be greater, and yet the love of David could not be more tender. He is obliged to march at the head of an army against this unnatural son, and to fight with him a decisive battle. But his greatest care before the engagement was urgently to exhort his officers and soldiers to save his son. This ambitious prince, cruel, ungrateful, perfidious, and most criminal, is the same son that David still loves, and that he desires to save, though he cannot do it but at the probable expense of his crown, and at the risk of his life. However, as we know, this son perished in the battle. David triumphs over the rebels, but the king is insensible to his victory, and is touched only at the death of his son. He forgets that this death delivers him from the most unworthy son that ever lived, that it restores to him his kingdom, and that it puts his life in safety. He forgets, I say, all these advantages, to think only of the loss that interests his heart. He sheds torrents of tears; he covers his face so as not to see the light of day; he moves all his court by his tearful cries; he would have sacrificed his kingdom and his life as well to save this unhappy son. "O my son Absalom, Absalom my son, who would grant that I might die for thee, Absalom my son, my son Absalom?" (2 Kings xviii. 23). Such are the sentiments of tenderness which God, our Father, has for us, even when sin puts us in a state of rebellion against Himself. In fact, it is the sinner who is figured by the ungrateful Absalom, and the sin of this prince has nothing in it more hateful than is found in the rebellion of him who violates the Will of God. But if such a sinner is as criminal as Absalom, God is not less tender than David. For what anxiety is there in this amiable God, "the Father of your life!" (Ecclesiast. xxiii. 24). What anxiety does He not manifest for the preservation, for the life, of the sinner, of whom the whole universe demands the punishment and death! I imagine I hear Him crying out to all the enemies of our life, "Save my son Absalom! spare his life!" Alas! on such and such an occasion, by sickness or by an accident, I thought to have died. I was then in the state of sin, and if I had died, I should have been lost for all eternity. But my God, and my Father! you are anxious for my life, for my salvation, and in the solicitudes of your tenderness, You ordered Your creatures to succour me. You sent Your angels to protect me; You said, "It is My son, it is My son Absalom, save him, save him whom I love."

It is thus that God loves the sinner. I add also, that we may say, in a certain sense, that He is interested in thus loving the sinner. I beg the reader to observe how sinners, however unworthy they may be, are useful to His glory. In truth, without the excess of their impiety, should we fully know the magnificence of His mercy, and without their wickedness would His mercy be manifested to us in its fullest extent? No—certainly, no. What has given Almighty God, therefore, an occasion of manifesting His goodness, is the malice of mankind; thus, according to the prophet Isaias, it is in the pardon He grants to sinners that He finds His own glory, "Therefore the Lord waiteth that He may have mercy on you, and therefore shall He be exalted sparing you" (Isaias xxx. 18), and the prophet adds elsewhere, that if God pardons the sinner, it is not only for the sinner's advantage, but He does it for His own sake, and for the sake of His own glory. "I am He that blotteth out thy iniquities for My own sake" (Isaias xliii. 25). It is by this thought that we may explain a remark of St. Paul, which seems somewhat obscure: "For all have sinned," he says, "and do need the glory of God" (Romans iii. 23). What is the glory of which the apostle speaks? It is that glory which a God of mercy finds in pardoning. It is glory to a king to punish, but it gives him glory also to remit the punishment. If it gives him glory to subdue and to humble those who rebel against him, it would be unworthy of his majesty and of his courage to exercise his severity on those who have recourse to his clemency. Such is the majesty of our God. All have sinned, all have revolted, all have deserved to be punished by His justice. How can they avoid it, since it gives His justice glory to humble and to punish them? It was necessary, then, that God should be glorified also in forgiving them. It is this glory of the mercy of God which becomes for us a principle of salvation, and a ground of hope. In this sense it is that sinners have need of the glory of God to receive the pardon of their sins.

From all that I have said, it is easy to conclude that though we are sinners, we must not suppose that therefore God has thoughts, in our regard, of vengeance and of hatred. It is the miserable, and sinners, who are the objects of His mercy—the property of this attribute is to pardon. Now who are they whom mercy pardons? Are they the innocent? Are they not rather the culpable, who, humbled after their sins, bring to this tribunal, as their sole claim the humble avowal of their misery, and the sincere desire to be delivered from it? It is upon them, then, upon the guilty, who are penitent, that His mercy displays most gloriously its power. "For this cause," says St. Paul, speaking of his conversion, "have I obtained mercy, that in me first Christ Jesus might show forth all patience, for the information of them that shall believe in Him unto life everlasting" (1 Tim. i. 16). All sinners would feel, as St. Paul, the effects of the mercy of God, if they brought no obstacle to it by their distrust or by their presumption. Once more, then, it is not being a sinner, nor a great sinner, that is an obstacle to the mercy of God. It seems, on the contrary, that it is a still stronger motive for hope. A prince has founded a magnificent hospital; all the poor, without exception, are received into it, and treated with care and with love. The sick, the lame, those who are covered with ulcers and with rags, do they despair of admittance because of their misfortunes and their misery? Do they not, on the contrary, count on their rags, and their ulcers, and on their infirmities, as a reason to be received? Do they think that the gate of a house destined to receive all the miserable, would be closed to the most miserable of all? It is thus that the number and enormity of my sins should not discourage me from hoping in the mercy of God, just as this poor man covered with ulcers is not discouraged by his misery from applying for entrance into the hospital founded for that very intention to receive such applicants as himself. However great, then, are my sins, far from their excluding me from the mercy of God, they give me, on the contrary, the right to claim and to invoke it; *because* they are so very great and without number, *therefore* it is that I say the more readily as well as earnestly, "my God, save me, deliver me. If I am the greatest of all sinners, it is in saving and delivering me, O Lord, that You manifest the great extent of Your mercy, and the power of Your redemption."

CHAPTER XI.

GOD CALLS THE SINNER, AND EVEN HIS THREATS IN CALLING HIM, SHOULD RATHER EXCITE OUR CONFIDENCE THAN DISCOURAGE OUR WEAKNESS.

GOD loves the sinner, sinner as he is. If we still doubt this truth, let us think with what goodness He calls him in his sinful wanderings, in order to lead him to Himself. We have shown this at length, and we will not repeat here what we have already said. Observe only that they whom He has come to seek, are sinners; they for whom He died, are sinners; they whom He calls, are sinners; they whom He presses the most earnestly to come to Him, are the greatest sinners; they whom He urges the most strongly, after whom He calls the most loudly, they who are at the greatest distance from Him. To have sinned, to have sinned much, to have committed enormous sins; this then is no reason for thinking that He will reject you, if you wish to give up your sins. How can we imagine that what constitutes the matter of mercy, and is its very object, should become an obstacle in its way, and cool it in our regard? It is true that our God gets weary of calling with sweetness sinners who are insensible to His caresses; He therefore threatens and reproaches them. All Holy Scripture is full of these threats and menaces. But is there anything in this, which should hinder us from going to Him with confidence? Certainly not! on the contrary it is this, which discovers to us still more clearly, the repugnance He has to punish us. For to utter complaints, reproaches and threats —this is not the language of an irritated God who does not pardon. It is not thus that true and real anger speaks by the mouth of one, who has the power to punish. It is after dissembling, and silence, that vengeance comes, like the lightning from the dark cloud. To threaten is to give notice, to put off, it is to give time to avoid the punishment. Is not this an effect of His mercy?

This is what is clearly taught us in the history of the conversion of the Ninevites. Who would not have thought that God in His anger had resolved upon their destruction, when a Prophet was sent to them, to signify to them expressly the decree of Almighty God—"yet forty days and Nineve shall be destroyed" (Jonas iii. 4).

How long was it, then, before the destruction was to come upon the city and on its inhabitants? It was not in a century, in a year, but after the short delay of forty days. The Prophet does not say, do penance in order to avoid the coming ruin, perhaps you may obtain mercy—or, your city will be wholly destroyed unless you do penance—no! it is not thus that he speaks; the judgment appears absolute, the sentence irrevocable—"yet forty days and Nineve shall be destroyed." The people of the city believe that it will be so; and if they do penance, it is with a doubt of its success, in turning away the wrath of God. "Who can tell, they said, if God will turn and forgive?"—this "who can tell," this doubt, this uncertainty, is a sufficient motive for doing penance—but, after all, it is only a doubt, and they dare not assure themselves positively of pardon.

The Prophet himself did not believe that

they would obtain it. He waited to see the accomplishment of his prophecy, and not daring after his preaching, to remain in the city, for fear of being buried himself in its ruins, he retired to a tree outside the gates, and waited under its shadow to witness the vengeance of God. But how is it, O Prophet, that you do not know the mercies of God, who threatens us through His infinite goodness? Is it likely that if He had resolved to destroy this city without remission, that He would have sent you to warn its inhabitants? There is here a lesson that God wished to give Jonas himself; and taking occasion from the vexation of the Prophet at the decay of the ivy which God had given him for a shade, He said to Jonas, "Dost thou think that thou hast reason to be angry on account of the ivy ?—thou art grieved for its decay, the decay of that for which thou hast not laboured, nor made it to grow, which in one night came up, and in one night perished. And shall I not spare Nineve, that great city in which there are more than one hundred and twenty thousand (infants) that know not how to distinguish between their right hand and their left, and many beasts?" (Jonas iv. 10, &c.); as much as to say, the inhabitants of this great city are My creatures, they belong to Me, they are My children—it is I Who have given them life—how then shall I fail to be touched by their humiliations? I have threatened them only that they might do penance; since they have done it, what can I desire more than their obedience?—shall I destroy a people docile and humbled?

It is thus that God is merciful even in His threats, in His menaces, and in His reproaches. He is so for all sinners. It is with sincerity that He calls them, and that He fears to be obliged to punish them. To have sinned greatly, is not then a reason for believing that we shall have no share in His mercy.

A touching example of what I have just said, I call here to mind; we find it in an ancient author, and it is very apposite to our subject.

CHAPTER XII.

CONFIRMATION OF THE FOREGOING. IMAGE OF THE TENDERNESS WITH WHICH GOD SEEKS THE SINNER, ACCORDING TO A HISTORY RELATED BY AN ANCIENT AUTHOR (VALERIANUS MAXIMUS).

THERE was once a father, who was unhappy in his only child. His unnatural son, without any reason for discontent, resolved to assassinate his father. He sought an opportunity of committing this dreadful crime. The father having learned the son's intention, hid one day a dagger in his breast, and begging his son to accompany him, he led him into a solitary place, in the depth of a thick forest, where the light of day could scarcely penetrate. Then seeing himself alone with his wicked son, he drew his dagger. His son, astonished at this sight, thought immediately that it was all over with his life, and his conscience accusing him of his criminal intentions, he concluded that his father had led him to that solitary spot, out of revenge, and the more easily to take away his life. Such was not the design of this good father. "My son," he said to him, "take this dagger, and since you are so determined to take away my life, satisfy here your desire in safety. Here is my heart, plunge this dagger into it—let your parricidal hand not spare me; I will not resist. I have led you into this solitude, that in offering you my life, I might save yours, and preserve your honour as well. You will not have occasion to hire an assassin, nor to prepare a poison; take away then without peril to yourself, the life of one who has given you so much displeasure. If a blind fury has made you forget that you are my son, I will not forget that I am your father. I wish that you should owe to me a second time the life that I am now saving from the hands of executioners, by sacrificing for you my own, in this solitary place. Once more, my son, my dear son, however cruel is your desire, gratify it, for I must die soon, either by your cruelty, or through my own sorrow; in dying here, I shall have the consolation of hiding in darkness the shame of your parricide, and I shall give you once more this mark of my tenderness, to which you ought to have been more alive."

This unnatural son, though so hardened, was moved by these words. He threw himself immediately at the feet of his father, and overcome both by the shame of his intended crime, and by the admirable goodness of his father, he tried in vain to make a reply. His sobs and tears stifled his words; hardly could he utter a few syllables, which were nearly choked by his sobs: "Live, my dear father, live, it is I that should die. I have well deserved my death. Turn that dagger against me; I cannot any longer endure the light, having so deliberately thought of committing so great a crime. Bury for ever in this spot the shame of my cruel designs; if your hand does not permit you, I must...." He could not finish the sentence, his redoubled sobs entirely choked his words; the father sobbing also, threw himself on the neck of his son, transported with joy to find him so moved and so changed. Compelling him to rise, they were for a long while unable to speak to one another but by their tears.

That this son was touched by the charming goodness of his father we are not surprised;

but what should we have said if insensible to all the sentiments of our nature, and to satisfy his wrath, he had seized the poniard which his father had presented to him? Should we have found terms in which to express the shame of his ingratitude, and indignation at the cruel parricide? Alas! let us moderate our anger, let us stay our indignation, or, rather, let us turn them against ourselves. Alas! this crime we commit every day. I recognize in the tenderness of this good father that of Jesus Christ, Who has graciously offered us His life, in order to manifest to us His love, and to excite our own. But I do not recognize in our own conduct the conversion of that unnatural son. Instead of being touched by the tenderness of so good a God, how often do we add each day more crimes to those which brought Him down upon this earth! He offered Himself to mankind, in order to die for them, and man has satiated upon Him all His fury. Not content with this barbarity, by every mortal sin which we commit, "we crucify again to ourselves the Son of God." He presents Himself often to us; He speaks to us, He presses us, He puts Himself into our hands, and from all these merciful advances He derives no other fruit but contempt and insult. Is not this to take the dagger from the hand of His Father, and to plunge it into His Heart? Who would not think that this Father (I would call him almost too good), ought to be irritated with such ingratitude? But we have not reached the term of Almighty God's tenderness for sinners. So merciful in calling them in their wanderings, He is also patient in awaiting their delays.

CHAPTER XIII.

GOD HAVING SPOKEN IN VAIN, MERCIFULLY CONDESCENDS TO WAIT STILL LONGER FOR THE RETURN OF THE SINNER. HOW ADMIRABLE THIS PATIENCE IS; THE CONSEQUENCE HE OUGHT TO DRAW FROM IT.

GOD waits for the sinner, and it is for this reason, that He is as slow to punish as He is prompt to pardon. "Man," says St. Chrysostom admirably, "is long in doing a work, and he is diligent and quick in destroying it. Almighty God, in the work of His grace, acts in quite a different manner. He is prompt in creating, He is prompt also to purify and pardon. An instant sufficed Him to create, man, to sanctify St. John, to convert St. Paul, to touch Mary Magdalen, to pardon the good thief. But must He punish? One might almost say that He forgets He has the power to act: He defers, He waits, He threatens, He dissembles, He seems almost not to know our sins. If He is at length obliged to punish, He puts off still longer the time of punishment, either to show us the regret He has to punish, or to give us an opportunity, on this fresh delay, of turning aside His anger. He has resolved to punish man by the deluge. He has determined to destroy him from off the face of the earth, which he had defiled by his abominations. He is a hundred years in threatening him: He wishes to punish Nineve for its crimes. After a thousand delays He issues the final sentence, but He defers its execution for forty days. He would punish the Jewish people by the captivity; several centuries pass in giving them warnings. He is busy all this time in speaking to them by a hundred prophets. He rises early in the morning, in order to urge them to do penance. "I have sent to them all my servants, the prophets, rising early and sending them" (Jeremias xxxv. 15). He is like a man in earnest who fears a misfortune, and who interrupts his sleep to search for a fitting remedy. Such is the patience of Almighty God in waiting for the conversion of sinners.

Here is, then, another characteristic of Almighty God's goodness for the sinner, so capable of comforting him in his distrust, that I fear lest he should draw from it too much assurance to continue in sin. Is it not great goodness to await the doing penance on the part of one who has hitherto abused all the graces he has received for that intention? What is it to await the sinner? It is to suffer patiently his insults, and the unworthy preference he gives to creatures. To wait for the sinner is to give him time to be a sinner, and to aggravate his sin. To wait for the sinner, O my Saviour, is to risk Your own glory, and all the fruit of Your passion. Is there anything that can better manifest Your tenderness for sinners? Certainly it is not from want of power that Almighty God acts with sinners thus; on the contrary, it is because He is infinite in His power, that He seems afraid or unwilling to exercise it, and that He keeps it back, to give time and space for penance. "But Thou hast mercy upon all, because Thou canst do all things, and overlookest the sins of men, for the sake of repentance" (Wisdom ii. 24). Great power is, ordinarily speaking, among men, a reason for having no pity, but in Almighty God it is a reason for sparing and accommodating Himself to the feebleness of His creatures. Now what greater patience, or what greater goodness can there be, than to have the power of punishing the sinner without difficulty, without risk, without injustice, without responsibility, and yet to spare him, even in the midst of his insults and his injuries. Saul understood that David truly loved him, when he knew that this holy man, whose life he endeavoured continually to take away, had had it in his power to take revenge by putting him to death, and yet had spared him. Saul is moved at this, and shed tears. He calls David his son, he blesses him, and says to him with astonishment, "I see clearly that you love me, and that my life is precious in your sight, since you have spared me, when you had so good an opportunity of depriving me of life." In fact, who "when he has found his enemy, will let him go away?" (1 Kings xxiv. 20). May we not say the same of Him of Whom David was a figure, and Who is a thousand times more merciful than David? How comes it, O my Saviour, that You suffer me with so much patience, and spare me for so long a time? I am in Your hands, and it was always in Your power to destroy me. It is Your long suffering, O my Lord, which makes me understand what confidence I ought to have in Your mercies. If You have been so good to me whilst I irritated You by my sins, what will be Your tenderness now that I return to You, and that I try to appease You by my tears? In truth, when I think, on the one hand, of the stupidity of man, who dares to insult his God, and on the other, God's patience, Who feigns not to notice these insults, it seems to me that I see a little child in the arms of its mother. This child having no power of reason, is sometimes in bad humour; it is impatient and irritable; it cries, and strikes with its little hands the breast of its mother who carries it, and it does its best to satisfy its feeble anger. What vengeance will the mother take of the angry petulance of her little one? She presses it more tenderly to her heart; she redoubles her caresses, she flatters it, she offers it her breasts and her milk to appease it. This is all the vengeance she takes. If this infant had sense and knowledge, what would be its thoughts on seeing so much tenderness? Give it for a moment the use of reason which nature has denied it, what would it think, what would be its sentiments, when its anger had passed away? Would it not be astonished at the bold rashness with which it had been irritated against its mother, who held it in her arms, and who had only to open them, for it to be dashed against the ground? At the same time, would it fear that this good mother would refuse to pardon its little furies? Would it not see, on the contrary, that they are already pardoned, since she caresses it so tenderly, while yet she is able to avenge herself on it so easily?

It is thus that God holds us in His arms; it is thus that He treats us; it is thus that He caresses us, in the midst of our strange and unruly passions. In order that we may have no doubt about it, it is He Himself Who has dictated this comparison to His Prophet Osee, (xi. 1). "Because Israel was a child, and I loved him," and again to the Prophet Isaias (xlvi. 3). "Hearken to me, O house of Israel, who are carried by My bowels, and borne by My womb, even to your old age I am the same, and to your gray hairs I will carry you. I have made you, and I will bear; I will carry, and will save you;" and again (Isaias xlix. 15), "Can a woman forget her infant, so as not to have pity on the son of her womb? and if she should forget, yet will I not forget you." Let us learn then to make a suitable return for so great a goodness. Let the tenderness of our confidence, answer to the tenderness of His love. Sinners as we are, let us address ourselves to Him with a lively hope in His goodness, since He not only awaits, and threatens, and caresses the sinner, but He receives him with mercy on his return. It is the fourth characteristic of the goodness of our God toward sinners, one that is so well calculated to give additional comfort to those whom the fear of His anger has thrown into discouragement.

CHAPTER XIV.

FOURTHLY. ALMIGHTY GOD RECEIVES THE SINNER WITH KINDNESS THE MOMENT HE RETURNS TO HIM.

How is it possible that Almighty God should not receive sinners on their repentance, whom He loaded with so many blessings in their impenitence? Your sins are numerous, it is true, they are very great, you who have been stagnant in them for so long a time; but are they more hateful to your God now that you detest them, that you groan under them, that you fear His wrath for them, than they were when you loved them more than Himself, and when by them you insulted His mercy? He knew then all their malice and all their enormity, and yet He endured you so patiently—will He be inexorable, now that you condemn yourself and your criminal attachments, with all your heart ? Then you offended Him, with deliberate purpose, with reflection, with malice —and He loved you, He sought you, He called you, He loaded you with benefits even when you were unconscious of them, and even when He foresaw the abuse you would make of His graces. Then, I say once more, He loved you, and His love for you was great. If benefits are a proof of love, great benefits are a proof of great love. By these benefits He bestowed upon you, I judge that He loved you greatly, tenderly, constantly. How then has it come to pass that to-day He has ceased to love you ?—to-day, that you are submissive and penitent, that you humble yourself at the view of His judgments, and that you humble yourself under the load of your sins ? Is it possible, that on account of this holy change in your dispositions and conduct, that He has thoughts of anger in your regard, of chastisement and of reprobation ? Could Almighty God possibly entertain such thoughts ? Would it not be making your God a God Who acts strangely, and even with injustice, one who loves the impious and rejects the penitent?

No, doubtless, He will not reject returning sinners—and if we consider well His designs, we shall find that the reason which engages Him to wait for the sinner, engages Him also to receive him. St. Peter teaches us this, when he says, "The Lord dealeth patiently for your sake, not willing that any should perish, but that all should return to penance" (2 Peter iii. 9).

No, Almighty God does not wish that any sinner should perish; on the contrary, He wishes that he should not perish. He wishes that all should desire their own conversion and salvation; He wishes it, He longs for it, He is afflicted when sinners do not answer to His desires, He waits, as if He would see whether they would not be moved at last, to repent. What greater joy for Him Who thus desires our salvation, than to see His wishes accomplished, and His care rendered fruitful, by the return of those whose conversion He is so anxious to bring about?

It is not then the character of our God, to reject the sinner on his return, after having spared him in his wanderings. I imagine Him saying with kindness to each of us, what the Patriarch Joseph said formerly to his brethren in order to comfort them in their fright, at the moment when they recognised him in Egypt—"I am Joseph, your brother, whom you sold into Egypt: be not afraid" (Gen. xlv. 4).

His brethren, who in their cruelty had conspired together against him, and in selling him to strangers had delivered him up to all the miseries that accompany slavery, his brethren, I say, surprised to see their younger brother so mighty, and the master of all the empire of Pharaoh, were affrighted at the remembrance of the bad treatment they had shown him—"He will remember the wrong he suffered, they said one to another, after the death of our father, and he will requite us all the evil we did to him" (Gen. l. 15).

Beautiful image of the alarm of the sinner at the hour of death, when he considers as now so near to him, the majesty and the power of God, whom he had forgotten during the course of a sinful life.

Yet Joseph has much more noble sentiments than his brethren feared they should find in him. He penetrates their anxiety, and before they ventured to speak to him, he anticipates them—they had not yet asked his pardon, and already he has forgiven them. He is the first to speak to them, and in these consoling words: " Do not be afraid, I am Joseph, your brother. I have forgotten all the past, do you forget it also, and be of good comfort; come near to me that I may embrace you. I will only revenge myself upon you by my embraces. Cease then, for the future, to have any fear; your fear will be injurious to my friendship. I am your brother, and I shall be always your brother by my affection, the same as I am your brother by nature."

Of all the figures of Jesus Christ in the Old Testament, I do not find one so touching as that of the Patriarch Joseph. Jesus Christ was like Joseph in the persecution which his brethren raised against him—in the treason with which they sold him, in his slavery, in his prison. He was a still more perfect type of the Saviour, in his glory and in the salvation of Egypt. But, to my own mind, the closest resemblance to the Holy Patriarch, is in his tenderness to his brethren, who so little merited it. It is thus, O divine Saviour, that You treat us, and if we are as culpable in Your regard as the brothers of Joseph were towards him, You are not the less tender and merciful, than this Patriarch, since he was a figure, in a particular manner, of Yourself. How shall I not then comfort myself in my sins? You say to me still more tenderly than Joseph did to his brothers, "I am your brother, do not be afraid." But why not fear? Because I am your brother, and I should be an unnatural brother, if I sought to avenge myself. If you were not penitent, I should be your judge, but since you return to me, I have no other quality in your regard than that of brother, nor have I any other dispositions in your regard, but those of friendship and tenderness.

CHAPTER XV.

CONTINUATION OF THE SAME SUBJECT. HOW GOD RECEIVES SINNERS. PARABLE OF THE PRODIGAL SON. IMAGE OF OUR MISERY IN THIS LIBERTINE.

SUCH is the tenderness with which Almighty God receives the sinner. It is thus that He comforts him in his fear; but in order to omit nothing that might inspire us with the confidence which He knows is so necessary for us, He has pointed it out to us still more clearly in the Parable of the Prodigal Son. Who is this father, asks Tertullian, this father so merciful and so ready to pardon, and who receives his son with so much kindness? It is without doubt our God, Who is more our Father than all the fathers of the earth, Who is more merciful than all the merciful on the earth. But before we recognize in this figure the mercies of our God, let us begin by seeing our own wanderings typified in those of the Prodigal Son. First, I see that among the children of this good father it was the youngest that rose up against him. It is the lot of the young not to suffer restraint; they would be their own guides; they do not listen to advice, they are inconsiderate and rash, and follow blindly their passions. The youngest son demands of his father the portion of his substance that was kept in reserve for him. It was not yet time for him to have and to enjoy it. He ought to have deserved it by services rendered to his father; and while he waited for the day to come, he should have been contented with the little liberalities that an indulgent father gives to his children, while he husbands the capital of his property that it might increase, and one day make his children rich. But this son would not await a solid happiness that was preparing for him, he would much rather have a portion of the property coming to him, than to preserve the certain right to great possessions hereafter. It is a symbol of our unworthy choice, in preferring the actual and present enjoyment of the miserable joys of earth, to all the happiness of that rich inheritance which God, our Father, has destined for us hereafter in heaven. These passing and earthly joys are only a portion or part, and a very small part, too, of what is destined for us in heaven. However, it is for this little portion that we give up our right and claim to the eternal riches of our heavenly inheritance.

The father then gives to his son what he demanded of him. Indignant at the conduct of this rash youth, he might have immediately driven him from his house, but he could not make up his mind to do this, and if I correctly read his heart, I see that he would rather that his son should not quit the paternal roof. But this ungrateful son finds the presence of his father too troublesome and too annoying. He flies from him, and to avoid his admonitions, "He goes abroad into a far country." But what had his father done that he should flee away thus, and despise his tenderness? Alas! nothing at all to deserve such an act. It was not his father's reproaches, nor his punishments which drove away this unnatural son. It seems that this good father could not make up his mind to do without him, since he grants him, without delay, what he asks; and we, when we abandon ourselves to these criminal and earthly pleasures, when we fly from our God and banish ourselves from His Presence, is it for having received at His hands any cruel or hard treatment? What ingratitude to fly from Him "Who giveth abundantly to all, and upbraideth not" (St. James i. 5).

On this unhappy separation from his father, what does this imprudent son do? Soon he lost all, he wasted all. "He wasted his substance in riotous living." And we, when we precipitate ourselves into the abyss of sin, what becomes of all those pleasures which we thought to taste? How long do they last? A moment—fatal moment! which is followed by lasting regrets, by disgust, by bitterness, by vexation, by infirmities, and sometimes by despair. But what becomes of that portion of graces, of spiritual blessings with which our Father had enriched us? All is wasted! hardly there remains the salutary remorse of a troubled conscience, reproaching itself for its disorders, and which seems, of all the blessings we have wasted, to continue with us, only to avenge their loss.

See, then, the shame of your misconduct, so similar to that of the Prodigal Son. But our return is not the less like to his, and it is important to reflect upon it, in order to understand better the mercy of God our Heavenly Father in receiving us. First, it is only after long delays—perhaps after several years—that we return to God, as travellers who, after long journeys, return at length to their own country, which they seemed to have left for ever. Thus it was with the Prodigal in the Gospel. After he had witnessed many years of abundance and scarcity, he entered into himself. But why did he thus enter into himself? It is necessity that compels him. He is dying of hunger, he has no longer any resource left; and we, let us acknowledge it, when we return to God, is it of our own full and free consent? Is it not rather some contempt on the part of the world, the infidelity of friends, the loss of property, of reputation, of patrons, the pains of an infirmity, which consumes us by little and little; is it not one or other of these causes which compels us to have recourse to our Heavenly Father, when all else have abandoned us? The Prodigal Son makes at last a courageous resolution: "I will arise and go to my father." The resolution is followed by action. He leaves the farm, and sets out upon his journey home. See, he now nears his father's house, but will he venture to appear before his father, before his brother, before the domestics of the house, in the sad state to which he is reduced? I represent him to myself as one of those miserable beggars whom hunger has disfigured, and poverty has stripped—he has on only rags, and they but half cover him, and are continually dropping off, and are going in shreds. He scarcely lives by the help of an alms which his importunity forces from passers-by. Would it not make his father more angry to present himself to him in this state? Would it not also be difficult to recognize him? Alas! we know it; when our soul returns to God in the beginnings of penance, it is still more horrible in His eyes, and the stains of sin are a thousand times more frightful than the horrors of poverty.

But will not the Prodigal have something to

present to his father to appease him? Out of all the property he had received from him, will he have nothing to remit into his hands? At least, will he not find some excuse to palliate his conduct, and to render him less criminal in his father's eyes? Is there not some motive of interest by which he may engage his father to receive him?

Is there not yet in his inheritance some right left, that he may sacrifice to him, to appease his wrath? There is nothing at all—he owns it himself, "I am not worthy to be called thy son, make me one of thy hired servants, who gain their livelihood by the sweat of their brow. As to excuses, he has none, he does not seek any. He is prepared to say, in all simplicity, that he is the most culpable of all men—that heaven itself ought to interest itself to punish him. He has only his tears to present to his father. Such is the misery and poverty to which sin has reduced us. We have no merits, nor excuses, nor riches to present, all is reduced to tears—it is our only resource! But this resource appears to us to be a very little thing; behold what fills us with fear! How, we say, will a few tears be able to wash out so many sins? How will our Heavenly Father be contented with a few tears? How will He receive them? How will He pardon us? Let us silence our distrusts—they are injurious to our God. If we know the poverty and misery and the malice of our heart, let us learn to know the goodness of His own. If we have only tears to offer him, He asks nothing else, and already He has anticipated them, to come to us. Let us study, in order to recognize Him, the whole conduct of this good father in the Gospel, whom we know to be His type and figure.

CHAPTER XVI.

CONTINUATION OF THE SAME PARABLE. IMAGE OF THE GOODNESS OF GOD IN THAT OF THE GOOD FATHER WHO RECEIVED HIS PRODIGAL SON.

THE prodigal was yet a great way off from the house, when his father saw him. I admire the vigilance of this good father, whom I represent to myself in great disquiet at the prolonged absence of his son. He goes out often, and looks on all sides, to try if he could see him. He sees him at last—love guided his eyes, and enables him at that great distance to recognize the one for whom he sighed. Without that, how could he have recognized him so far off, and so disfigured, that no one else would have known him, though close to him? He sees his son, and his heart is moved —and with what is he moved? is it with indignation and anger? These sentiments would have been just, but they are not those of this good father. If he is moved, it is not with anger; it is not even with the pity that we might have for a miserable creature, in whom we felt otherwise no interest. He is moved "with compassion," says the parable, with a tenderness such as a mother feels for the child she has carried in her womb. He runs therefore to him, to anticipate his approach. But what is this father thinking of? the gravity of his character as a father, the weight of his years, ought they not to keep him back? Besides, is he sure that his son is penitent, and that he does not come to insult him? But if he wishes only to listen to his tenderness would he not be doing enough to walk a few steps towards his libertine son? is it necessary that he should run to him? Has he not to fear that he might commit himself, and lower his dignity as a father, in thus humbling himself to anticipate one, to whom he would be showing favour enough, in simply receiving him? Besides, would it not be more fitting for him to dissemble his joy, that his son might the better understand all the enormity of his fault, and that he might purchase the pardon that he came to ask? Poor reflections of human prudence, to which true tenderness never listens! The tenderness of this good father is above and beyond all such considerations! it transports him—he is no longer master of himself. He is out of himself for joy—he runs to his son; love guides his tottering feet, and strengthens his faltering steps—he falls upon his son's neck and kisses him. He has forgotten what he has done, he has forgotten it, only to remember that he is his son; he caresses him, he presses him to his heart—he weeps over him, without leaving him hardly the leisure to speak, to accuse himself, and to ask pardon; he gives him all his heart, and he sheds over him more tears of joy, than the contrition of this Prodigal makes him shed of sorrow. But would it not have been better, that this good father should have made his son some mild reproaches for his ingratitude? Such reproaches are not incompatible with tenderness. It is true that he might have made them, but there is still more of mercy in sparing him the shame, who was already filled with confusion. Jesus Christ, Who wished to animate our confidence by this parable, feared no doubt, that such reproaches, always humiliating, might intimidate our weakness, ready to take fright at the slightest difficulty. Instead therefore of stopping to make such just reproaches, this good father loads him with blessings. He is anxious to do this on the spot, without waiting till he had proved by some delay, his son's perseverance in good. He puts all the domestics of the house in motion to seek new clothes, to find a robe worthy of his birth, and to fetch him a valuable ring. He prepares for him a magnificent banquet. He sends for musicians; his friends and relatives are invited to come and share the joy of this amiable father—he imposes silence on his eldest son, who jealous of so many favours and honours, would recall the remembrance of his brother's excesses. But the good father wishes that they should be forgotten, as he forgets them himself. "My son," he said, "was dead, and he is risen again; he was lost, and is found." He does not say, "My son was a sinner, and he is converted; my son was disobedient, and is now submissive." No! he has forgotten his son's acts of disobedience, his criminal and debauched life. It seems as if he was simply an unhappy innocent, who had left his father—"My son," he said, "was lost, and is found."

It is useless to apply this parable in detail. It is enough that we all feel it. But if we feel the application, should we not feel also the confidence with which it ought to inspire us? In fact, if our sins are very great, are they greater than those of this unnatural and libertine son? We have been late in doing

Confidence in the Mercy of God.

penance—was it not so with him? It was perhaps only a necessity, an affliction, or some vexation, which has been the occasion or cause of our conversion. Did his return to his father's house proceed from any principle more noble and disinterested? We do not bring with us any merits in returning to God, had he anything to present to his father? The only claim he had upon him was that of being his son, and that of his confidence and sorrow; are not we, like him, the children of God?—already we feel a lively sorrow for having irritated Him—let us add, that we have also a great confidence in His mercy. Let us go to Him boldly, and we shall be received with as much kindness as this libertine was by his amiable father. It is thus that God receives all penitent sinners. It is thus that He pardons sinners, and it is this pardon which characterises His mercy towards us—of this I purpose to speak in the following chapter. Doubtless this fifth and last characteristic of His mercy is already sufficiently proved by what I have already said, since to receive the sinner with kindness, and to pardon him, is the same thing; but it is well to make on this pardon a few short reflections, which are too consoling to be omitted.

CHAPTER XVII.

THE FIFTH CHARACTERISTIC OF THE GOODNESS AND MERCY OF ALMIGHTY GOD TOWARDS SINNERS: IN RECEIVING THEM, HE PARDONS THEM.

IF we add to the parable I have just explained the examples of sinners whom God has pardoned, and whose histories are recorded in the Holy Scriptures, it seems to me that there will not remain in us any more distrust; and however culpable we may be, we shall be able to say with St. Bernard, "There is no wound so great and so mortal which cannot be healed by the mercy of God, and by the Blood of Jesus Christ."

Who was more culpable than Manasses, King of Juda? His abominations and his crimes were frightful and horrible: sorcery, magic, idolatry, immodesty, cruelty, and injustice.

We shall have a clearer conception of the impiety of this king, when we remember that, not content with having abolished the worship of God throughout his kingdom, to substitute for it that of the most infamous idols; not content with having slain the Prophets of the Law, he himself sacrificed his own children to the devil, and that he sacrificed them by fire, according to the barbarous custom of the idolators of that time. This king, abandoned by God, became a captive. They loaded him with fetters, and he was hurled to the bottom of a deep dungeon, and it was while he was in this misery that he began to turn his heart to God. He wept, and asked God for mercy, and this God of goodness and mercy listened to his cry, and graciously heard his prayer, and gave him back his throne and his power, of which his sins had deprived him.

Who was more wicked than Achab, King of Juda, another model of all kinds of abominations? the worship of Baal, the persecution of Elias, the massacre of the Prophets, the blood of Naboth, the fury of Jezebel his wife, make him sufficiently known. One day the king humbled himself at the voice of a Prophet who threatened him. He is sad and afflicted; he puts on a hair shirt, he walks with an air of deep contrition. Frail conversion, which did not last! yet it was agreeable enough to Almighty God, to obtain a delay of the chastisement with which He had threatened him. What sins were more crying than those of David? A double adultery, and an adultery rendered more criminal by treachery and by the murder of one who was innocent. Up to that time he was a Prophet and a Saint, but the more holy he had been, and the more favoured by God, the more enormous was his crime. What ingratitude in a man so favoured! But what scandal, to see a Saint become so criminal! What scandal to see him add hardness of heart to his crime! In fact, the King was nearly one year without coming to himself and without repentance. Already the fruit of his criminal adultery was born when the Prophet came to speak to him on the part of God. He had need then of a Prophet and an extraordinary mission in order to recall him to his duty. This Prophet speaks to him, and the King, as he listens, enters into himself, and acknowledges his sin. He said but these few words: "I have sinned," and immediately the Prophet adds on the part of God, "the Lord hath taken away thy sin," without making him any bitter reproaches. God pardons with promptitude the sinner who returns to Him, though after a long delay.

Such was the facility that God had to pardon, at a time which St. Cyprian calls a time of severity and of vengeance. What will He not do now in a time of mercy, and under a law, called by excellence, a law of grace? What has Jesus Christ not done to give us proofs of His infinite mercy? A sinful woman, by her abandoned life, is the scandal of Jerusalem; the Son of God grants her the pardon of her sins as soon as ever she begins to ask for it. Zachaus is a public usurer, and as soon as he resolved to restore the property he had acquired by injustice, from that moment, and before he has had time to carry out his resolution, his sin is remitted, and salvation enters his house. A woman is surprised in the act of adultery; she is brought to Jesus Christ, Who delivers her from the death she had merited, according to the law, and forgiving her sin, imposes no other penance on her than her own confusion, with the guarantee to sin no more. An infamous robber, after many crimes, is attached to a cross; he is ready to expire. At this last moment he has recourse to Jesus Christ. Jesus listens to him with mercy, and gives him a speedy entrance into His glory. "This very day," He says to him, "thou shalt be with Me in Paradise." It is true, that this robber was close to the Cross of Jesus—that Cross which has been to the whole world a source of salvation. It is true, that being so near to this salutary Cross, we are less surprised to see that he is the first to experience the effects of its power. But if we are even as culpable as was this favoured thief, what hinders us from approaching this blessed Cross, and to cast our eyes on Him Who died upon it, to merit for ourselves the pardon of our sins? "I have lifted mine eyes to the mountains whence help cometh to me." Let us lift up our eyes to this holy mountain, Christ on the Cross, whence help will be sure to come to us. Let us look on it at leisure—alas! what do we see? We behold a sight, the most fitted to excite a loving confidence in the hearts of all sinners, the Blood of a God which is shed for their salvation, the Heart of a God opened to show itself to us with all its tenderness. If you doubt still this tenderness of His mercy and His love, look on this Heart which shows you what He is. It has been opened only to make Himself known to us, and to give us confidence. Across its deep wound, it is easy for you to see this Heart, which has no movement but for you, and has no feeling for you but that of tenderness. It is there, adds St. Bernard, that I would retire; it is in this Heart opened for my salvation, that I would find a safe refuge against the wrath of my God; it is in Him I wish to put my confidence, and my confidence will then be solidly founded. It is true that my sins are great, continues this father so humble and so devout; they are but too great, so that my confidence is mingled with fear, but it is not a fear which brings with it trouble or desolation, because the Wounds of my Saviour give me comfort, for "He was wounded for our iniquities, and by His stripes we are healed." What wounds can my soul receive which may not be healed by His Precious Blood? What fear is there, or what desolation of spirit which may not be cured by its efficacy? The Wounds of my Saviour are the "great remedy for healing all the malignity of sin." Such were the sentiments of St. Bernard. What hinders us from finding with him the same consolation in our Blessed Saviour's Wounds?

CHAPTER XVIII.

SIXTHLY. GOD NOT ONLY PARDONS THE PENITENT SINNER, BUT HE APPEARS TO FAVOUR HIM MORE THAN THE JUST.

GOD then pardons penitent sinners all the enormity of their sins. We may almost say that He favours them more than the just—"I say unto you, there shall be joy in heaven upon one sinner that doth penance, more than upon ninety-nine just, who need not penance."

—These are the words of Jesus Christ Himself in the gospel (St. Luke xv. 7).

It seems also that He rewards them more liberally, and we see holy penitents more glorified on the earth by the prodigies that God works at their intercession, than others whose innocent life would appear to merit the greater distinction. The reason is, that the preference and the rank of the saints in the eyes of God, is measured by the fervour of their love. Therefore if by a greater love the penitent has the advantage of the just, we must not be surprised if he surpasses him in glory, which is nothing else than the reward of love. An edifying history which I shall now relate in a few words may help to confirm what I have just said.

Thais, known in ecclesiastical history by the fervour of her penance, was not less known previously in the world, by the disorders of her dissolute life. Never did any one carry effrontery and shamelessness to a greater extent. The holy old man, Paphnuce, inspired by God to labour for her conversion, went forth from the desert to seek this sheep who had gone astray, and to lead her back to the fold.

I will not say anything of the admirable, (more admirable than imitable) industry by which he sought to gain her to God. It is enough to add, that having happily engaged her to quit not only sin, but all the occasions of sin, he conducted her into the desert, and shut her up alone, in a cell of which he kept the key, leaving only a little opening, through which he furnished her with bread and water, which alone served her for nourishment. This holy sinner, touched with horror for her sins, submitted willingly to a most rude and severe penance, severe indeed to one who was accustomed to a life of pleasure, of delicacy, and of company. She lived a long time in this solitude, continually weeping for her past sins, and imploring the mercy of God. In her prayer she did not even dare to pronounce the Name of God; fearing to stain it, if pronounced by lips so impure, she said only, "O Thou Who hast created me, have pity on me."

Three years flowed on, without any relaxation of her austerity or cessation of her tears.

Almighty God, to whom her tears were so pleasing, wished to make her case known to a holy man named Paul, a disciple of St. Antony, who was called from his simplicity Paul the Simple, a quality as precious in the sight of God as it is contemptible in the eyes of the world. This holy man, being at his prayers, saw in spirit a throne which was being prepared in Heaven. The whole celestial court seemed anxious to adorn it. Its beauty and magnificence surpassed every thing one could imagine, and the angels seemed impatient to receive the happy mortal for whom so beautiful a throne was destined. "For whom is this throne?" said the holy man to himself; "is it not for my holy father St. Antony? for who could merit such great glory in Heaven, but he who has done such great things for God while on earth?" His mind was occupied with this thought, when an Angel approaching him, freed him from his anxiety, by telling him, "This glorious throne is destined for Thais, the sinner—she has merited it, by her penance, and by her tears."

CHAPTER XIX.

CONCLUSION OF THE SAME SUBJECT. TO BE TOO ALARMED ABOUT OUR SINS, IS SOMETIMES A REFINEMENT OF SELF-LOVE.

I BELIEVE that I have said enough to comfort the timorous, who, alarmed at the sight of their sins, abandon themselves to discouragement.

But before I pass on to another reflection, I must make known to these unquiet and timorous persons, a subtle snare laid for them by the Evil one, which it is not easy to perceive, because it is hidden under the deceitful appearance of a salutary contrition. Often these fears, these discouragements, these desolations, are less the effect of the holy sadness of penance, than of a subtle pride, which cannot bear the sight of its own imperfections. They are sad, they are afflicted, they are agitated, and that beyond measure—and for what? is it because God is offended? No—but because they are so imperfect, or rather because they do not see in themselves enough of perfection. The pride which loves to please itself with itself, cannot bear the sight of so much weakness and imperfection. He who retains still 'some remnants of this vice, which is ingrained into us from our birth, not only wishes to be perfect, but he wishes to enjoy the consolation of knowing that he is so, to see that he has some virtue, and that he is agreeable to God. With this secret desire, how can he bear the sight of his daily falls, and the remembrance of his old disorders?

Now, in this state, the heart, full of pride, is easily troubled and discouraged by the remembrance of its sins. It is afflicted on account of them—but it is an affliction of dejection and discouragement, which disgusts and gnaws the heart, and gives it no peace. Believing that it is penetrated by a lively contrition, in reality, it is sometimes only troubled by self-love, and by an interior sentiment that I venture to call spiritual ambition,—ambition which is often found in a heart from which all other ambition is banished. The Spirit of God is not in discouragement, nor in trouble. It is only the tempter that finds his advantage in the one state and in the other. The affliction and sorrow that are inspired by the Holy Spirit have something in them more courageous, more consoling, and more peaceable.

He who is led by the Holy Ghost, "the Comforter," regards his sins with humiliation and sorrow, but if he is confused, he is not discouraged. He is not more troubled than a gardener when he sees growing in his garden useless weeds. He labours promptly to root them up, but he is not discouraged. The true penitent is not more discouraged than the gardener; his faults seem even to increase his fervour, and to animate his confidence, by deepening his humility. If he afflicts himself for his sins, he accepts with a good heart the humiliation they cause him. Let the scrupulous then, and the timorous, pay attention to this truth. Let them avoid with care this rock I have now discovered to them. It is necessary also to warn them of another, which causes perhaps as many shipwrecks—of which I shall speak a little more at length, because the subject deserves it.

CHAPTER XX.

THE LAST OBJECTION OF THOSE WHO ARE DISTRUSTFUL—THE SMALL NUMBER OF THE ELECT; GENERAL REFLECTION ON THIS TRUTH.

WHATEVER confidence we may have in the mercy of God, although we know that it is far greater than even the enormity of our sins, yet there remains in the soul of the just a last subject of alarm. It is a fear, as fatal in its effects as any of the causes of dejection I have already named, and perhaps not so easy to calm. It is that alarming truth which the faith teaches us,—the small number of the elect. After all, we sometimes say, I know that the number of the elect is small; how then shall I dare to think that I am of that number? When I see all the disorders of my past life, and all my daily infidelities, have I not much reason to fear that I shall be among that large number of sinners whom God at the last day will condemn in His anger? Such is the temptation. It is easy to conceive into what dejection this thought is capable of throwing all such as indulge in it.

This temptation is not new. From the time of the apostles, there were those who were troubled by it; and it was to comfort them that St. Peter, in one of his Epistles, tells the faithful that, instead of being discouraged by the fear of not being among the predestinated, it was their duty, each of them, to labour the more, that by good works they might make sure their calling and their election, that is, their predestination (2 Peter i. 10).

The holy fathers, and the masters of the spiritual life, have renewed continually the exhortation of the apostle, and they have drawn from the truths of the faith many wise reflections, with a view of strengthening the faithful against this temptation, and of encouraging those whom it might deject. I limit myself, however, to one single reflection, which appears to me to be the most efficacious in giving comfort, and not only takes away from the temptation any cause of alarm, but teaches us to draw from it a motive of consolation.

It is true that the number of the elect is

very small—but are you discouraged by this truth? Reflect on all the reasons you have for believing that you are of this happy number, and then your fear will be changed into consolation. In fact, what have you to fear as to the small number of the elect, if you believe that you are of that number; that God cherishes you with that particular love which secures the salvation of the saints? How is this? it is by the happy linking together of the special graces which sustain and support them in the different conditions and in the various events of our human life. Assuredly, he who recognises this merciful attention over him, far from being troubled at the small number of the elect, ought, on the contrary, to derive from it the strongest consolation. Now it is this thought with which I would inspire every one of those whom the tempter endeavours to throw into discouragement and despair by means of the temptation of which I am speaking. I say boldly, there is no one among those who are thus tempted who does not find in his own heart, in the singular graces which he has received from Almighty

God, in the favours which He has shown him, in the sentiments with which He has inspired him, in the protection He has afforded him in dangerous occasions, and in all the other circumstances of his life,—there is no one, I say, among those thus tempted, who does not find in his life proofs, sufficiently strong, of this good will of Almighty God for him in particular—the good will and protection of that God, who, though merciful to all men, cherishes His elect with a special love, and conducts them to conversion and to final perseverance by the most certain and the surest ways.

I am not speaking now of the general assurance we all have that this God of goodness loves us all enough to save us, nor of our obligation to believe that He has a sincere desire for the salvation of all men; a desire which is followed by the powerful aid which renders possible our salvation and our perseverance. I do not speak, now, of the advantages we have had in participating of this help by means of the Sacraments, which have regenerated us in Him, reconciled us to Him, and nourished us with His precious Body; nor do I speak of the promises He has made us not to aandon us to temptations above our strength to bear, and to grant us easily and infallibly all that we ask in the Name of His Son, without excepting perseverance and salvation. I may well, however, stop here, and endeavour to show that these graces, though common to many, are yet particular to each of us, and proper to excite our confidence, since they place in our hands the infallible means of assuring our predestination, if we make use of them for the end for which they were destined.

CHAPTER XXI.

ANOTHER REFLECTION ON THE SAME TRUTH. CONFIDENCE IN GOD IS A MEANS OF ASSURING, IN SOME SORT, OUR PREDESTINATION.

I WILL not stay to consider another means which Almighty God has given us all, to make easy for each of us in particular, the success of our salvation. I cannot, however, dispense myself from saying one word in this matter, since it is necessary to my subject. What is this means? I have already hinted what it is, and I willingly repeat it here. It is our having the same confidence that we shall end well the great affair of our salvation, as we had when we began it, at our conversion.

This confidence is one of the most probable marks of predestination. We find it difficult to conceive this paradox, because we judge according to our feeble ideas, and according to what passes among ourselves, for with us hope and confidence do not always render our desires efficacious. But with Almighty God, and in the affair of our salvation, to hope with confidence, is not only to render easy our victory over obstacles, but it is to assure ourselves, in some sort, of the crown. Why is this? It is because God Himself has promised it, and His word, that word that endureth for ever, which cannot change, is engaged to it. "Know," saith the Holy Scripture, "that no one hath hoped in the Lord, and hath been confounded" (Ecclesiast. ii. 11); and again, "hope confoundeth not" (Rom. v. 5); and again, "none of those who wait on Thee shall be confounded" (Ps. xxiv. 3); and again, "Thou savest them that trust in Thee" (Ps. xvi. 7).

"We are saved," saith St. Paul, "by hope" (Rom. viii. 24).

The Royal Prophet, all penetrated with this assurance of hope, cried out with transports of joy, "To Thee, O Lord, have I lifted up my soul. In Thee, O my God, I put my trust, let me not be ashamed" (Ps. xxiv. 1).

Let no one be astonished that God has given so much efficacy to confidence. Confidence, as I have said, is inseparable from love. It is itself a sort of love, or it may be called the bridge from faith to love—if not love itself, it is the mark of the most tender and the most vehement of all loves. Now we know there is nothing impossible to love; it is love, then, which opens the gates of Heaven. How is it possible that the Almighty should resist such confidence? His glory, His love, His heart—are they not all interested in not deceiving them who trust fully in Him? A son says to his father, I have such confidence in you, that I leave with yourself the decision as to my vocation, my occupation, my marriage, and the inheritance you may leave me. A servant says to his master, I do not dream of making any fortune, but that which you may give me yourself. I will serve you faithfully, and I leave to your goodness the recompense for my work." A friend, associated with his friend in trade, says to him with confidence, "I leave with yourself the decision of the business between us. I count on your uprightness and equity, and I do not wish for any umpire between us but yourself." This friend, this master, this father, will they be insensible to a confidence so entire, if they are men of good will and probity?

If they are jealous of their reputation, and of their glory, will they not be urged, by the confidence placed in them, to do even more than might be expected of them? For myself, if I were in their place, I should be much moved by so great a confidence, and I should think that I was much more indebted to him who treated me in this manner, than to one who, distrusting my good heart, or my exactitude, should dispute with me on the terms of agreement, and who, disquieted every moment as to the object of his hopes, would be anxious to know if he had all the securities. In a word, I should believe my honour and my reputation interested in not disappointing the generous confidence that had been placed in my probity.

Is it, then, that our God knows less the interests of His glory, or that He is less jealous in its regard? If He is in truth jealous of His glory, as the Scripture asserts, "I will not give My glory to another" (Isaias xliii. 8), will He suffer that those who, full of a tender love, repose in His goodness, and who, instead of being unquiet about their predestination and their reward, say with the Royal Prophet, "The Lord ruleth me, and I shall want nothing, He has set me in a place of pasture" (Psalm xxii. 1); will He suffer, I say, such to be deceived in their holy confidence, and so be able to complain one day, that after they had counted on His promises, they found them vain?

This holy confidence, then, gives us a sort of security that we shall not be deceived, and that we shall succeed in the great affair of our salvation, since there is a question of the glory of God and of the truth of His word—and therefore it is that St. Paul exhorts his Hebrew converts "not to lose their confidence, which hath a great reward" (Heb. x. 35).

What great reward is this? it is the security of our salvation, since "we are saved by hope," that is, by our confidence in God, Who can never deceive or disappoint us. How, then, with a means in our hands so easy and so efficacious, can we doubt our predestination? Is it not a mark that we are of the number of those whom Almighty God has chosen, that He has made known to us a means so simple and so effectual of securing our salvation? Yet it is not at this reflection I wish to stop, nor to dwell upon its truth—the man who is unquiet and distrustful will say that these advantages of which I have now spoken are common to all the faithful, and that yet there are many to whom they are useless, and who perish.

CHAPTER XXII.

PRINCIPAL REPLY TO THE OBJECTION MENTIONED IN THE PRECEDING CHAPTER. THE SMALL NUMBER OF THE ELECT IS A CONSOLING TRUTH FOR THOSE WHO HAVE REASON TO THINK THEY BELONG TO THIS SMALL NUMBER. WHAT ARE THE MARKS OF PREDESTINATION. FIRST MARK, CHOICE AND VOCATION.

IN truth, what can any one say who continues obstinate in his distrust when we point out to him very many particular and personal graces which Almighty God has bestowed upon him all his life—graces which He gives him every day, and which He has not bestowed upon a multitude of others, and which appear to be the same as those He has granted to His chosen and to His elect, in order to conduct them by the way of penance and of perseverance to eternal life? Indeed, what is predestination but a choice that Almighty God makes of certain souls, whom, foreseeing their perseverance in grace, He leads by special helps to a crown prepared for them in

Heaven. What brings about this predestination? firstly, personal graces, particular helps proportioned to the different trials of life, and so disposed as to secure a final victory. Let us say very clearly and in three words—predestination implies, first of all, choice and vocation; secondly, conversion and protection, and thirdly, perseverance. "Whom God has predestinated," saith St. Paul, "them He also called, and whom He called, them He also justified, and whom He justified, them He also glorified" (Rom. viii. 30).

In these words, those of whom I speak will be able, no doubt, to recognize their own case, or rather the conduct of God in their regard. Is not this enough to make them hope to be of that small number of the elect, however small it may be? For as regards their vocation, and the choice God has made of them, could they be more clearly marked? In order to see this, compare your state with that of the infidels, schismatics, and heretics who cover the earth. The greatest part of the world is inhabited by those who live without faith, or who have not the true faith. Catholicity is professed by perhaps only the fifth or sixth part of the world; also many of those who live in countries where the Catholic religion is professed, may be described as dissolute—indevout—and even atheists—without the faith, even in the country of the faith! How many others are there, who, having nothing of the true religion but its belief, do not fulfil their obligations for want of that "faith which worketh by charity!" How many live in a profound ignorance of what they ought to know! How many others heap up their acts of injustice, and thus enriching themselves, put an obstacle in the way of their salvation, which they will never be able to remove! How many are guilty of committing those sins, of which the apostle says that they who do such things shall never enter the kingdom of Heaven! How many, without living very criminal lives, continue in forgetfulness of their salvation, and indifference about their eternal state! Take away nearly all these (if they do not do penance), take them out of the number of the predestinate. What will remain but a very small number of those who hold the faith, religion, piety, and justice in esteem; of those who are troubled about their salvation, and who work for it seriously; or, finally, of those who, after having given way too easily to temptations, to the "sin which surrounds us," according to the words of St. Paul (Heb. x. 1), wish to expiate their sins by penance. Now it is, without doubt, for this small number that Heaven is destined, and it is to this small number that Almighty God has called *you*. He has chosen you, in preference to a multitude of others, to place you in this company of His Elect. How many graces have you not received up to this moment, that you might be one of those blessed few! I do not speak of general and common graces, but of those graces of predilection; of those personal favours which have not been granted to all, as to you, and which show clearly the choice Almighty God has made of you for Heaven, and the particular desire He has to save you—to save *you*—though, which is impossible, He had abandoned all the rest of the world!

CHAPTER XXIII.

SECOND MARK OF PREDESTINATION. CONVERSION AND PARTICULAR PROTECTION.

To these distinguished graces of choice and vocation, which Almighty God has bestowed upon you, how many others has He added, as great and as special, for your conversion, your sanctification, your protection, and your defence! Repass in your mind all the years that have flown by; you will see in them a continuous chain of personal mercies, which has marked each moment of your life by singular graces prepared expressly for you, as if there had been no one else on the earth but yourself, to attract the attention and care of your God! Was it, then, to destroy you, to make you the victim of His anger, to reprove you in His indignation, that He has done for you what He has not done for millions of Christians, who would have valued these graces perhaps more than yourself?

When I recall to mind the years of my life which have passed away, the years of my childhood, of my youth, and of a riper age, I see a chain, as I have said, a continued series, of extraordinary mercies which I had in no way merited, so that I cannot doubt that this God of goodness had the design of leading me by a true conversion of heart to final perseverance, and from that to the crown destined for His Elect. After having preserved me in the womb of my mother, that I might not have an untimely death before I was baptised, after having been my God, as the Psalmist says, from my mother's breasts (Ps. xxi. 10), what care did He not take in my infancy to prepossess my young heart with the light of His grace, to arm me against the perils that then began to surround me! If I have had good parents, masters fearing God, an education wise and pious, it was His amiable Providence which had prepared for me this timely aid.

When my reason began to be developed, and I opened my eyes to know the world, what zeal, O my Saviour, did you not take to undeceive me, and to caution me beforehand against its seductions. Then what warnings, what secret instructions; what interior movements, what remorse I could not stifle! As I advanced in age, Almighty God multiplied His mercies in my regard. Sometimes He preserved my life from a fatal accident, which would have taken it away, and have delivered me to eternal flames! Sometimes He stopped me by unforeseen and unexpected disappointments, when, urged by my passion, I was on the point of abandoning myself to the deceitful charms of the world. Sometimes He mingled with my pleasures, vexations, and a mortal sadness, to wean me from them. Sometimes He spoke to me interiorly and pressed me to give myself to Him, making me hear in my heart all the tenderness and love for me which He had in His own, so far as I could share it.

If I saw fall around me the companions of my pleasures, by a sudden and unprovided death, it was You, O Lord, Who arranged for me, in Your love, this mournful sight, to teach me not to count on youth or life, and to make You in good time the sacrifice of a blessing You could take from me, as from them. If I saw others, more faithful to Your voice, quit the world to seek their salvation in the retreats of sanctity, You had me in view in these triumphs of Your grace, and You prepared for me their example to instruct and to touch me. If I found an emptiness in any pleasures, weariness in company, inconstancy in friends, perfidy in rivals, ingratitude in the masters I served, and severity and hardness in the patrons whom I reverenced, it was again You, O my Lord, Who sowed with thorns the path of perdition in which I was unconsciously walking, and Who acted thus to oblige me to turn myself to You, from Whom, without reflection, I was going far astray.

Would that I could count all the interior movements of Your Spirit, the secret warnings of Your grace, the pressing remorse of my conscience, the sweetness and the bitterness You have procured so seasonably for me to detach me from the world.

But, O my Saviour, have I not wearied Your patience by so many times not recognising or disregarding Your voice, so amiable and so sweet, which made itself heard in my heart? Have You not withdrawn that help, which Your liberal Hand poured forth so abundantly upon me? Without doubt I should have deserved this chastisement, and should have reason to fear that such is the case, did I not feel actually the same grace at work within me still as before, and which invites my heart, so often rebellious, with an ineffable sweetness. If this heart is sometimes affrighted at Your justice, I recognise in this fear also, the effect of Your mercy, since Your grace which creates these terrors within me, only makes me feel them, that I might become more vigilant and more faithful.

It is thus that we, each of us, should speak. I venture to assert that there is not one among those who shall read this Treatise, who, on recalling to mind the entire period of his past life, will not acknowledge in it—the evident marks of the predilection of God, and who will not be obliged to avow that he has received millions of singular graces, which all tended to bring about his true conversion, and to obtain more infallibly his salvation. Is it reasonable, after so many proofs, still to doubt the good will of Almighty God, and His predilection? Is it possible, in His conduct in our regard not to recognise the vocation added to choice, the conversion of life which followed the vocation, and the protection added to both, which, as I have said, are at once the effect and the means of predestination, and which, consequently, are its consoling marks. It is the road by which God has conducted the Saints—it is thus that He has treated them. He treats you as He treated them; He has chosen you as He chose them; He has sanctified you as He sanctified them; He will crown you as He has crowned them.

CHAPTER XXIV.

THIRD MARK OF PREDESTINATION. PERSEVERANCE IN GRACE. REASONS FOR HOPING IT. PROOFS OF PREDESTINATION TAKEN FROM THE TEMPTATION ITSELF TO DISCOURAGEMENT.

NOTHING more is wanted to finish the work of our salvation than a perseverance of mercy on the part of God, and a perseverance of fidelity on ours. But this is an additional reason for comfort. Although we cannot have an absolute certainty, without an express revelation, as St. Francis had, that we shall persevere to the end, yet how many reasons are there of hoping and conjecturing, with all the likelihood possible, that this merciful God will finish the work that He has commenced, as St. Paul says: "Being confident of this very thing, that He that hath begun a good work in you will perfect it unto the day of Jesus Christ" (Philipp. i. 6); that He will not abandon us to the fragility of our own inconstancy, and that He will sustain us to the end, as He has protected us hitherto. For He has placed us in the way, and this with infinite care and with admirable helps. Perhaps He has worked prodigies to place us there; is it likely that He will abandon us, and lose all the fruit of so much care and so much vigilance? He has put us in the way, and in what way? in the way in which He has placed His Saints who now triumph in Heaven. Is it possible that He has the design of destroying us, in the way by which He has conducted His Saints to triumph and to glory?

Ought I not to say to myself, if Almighty

God had wished to condemn and destroy me, would He have displayed for me so much goodness, so much predilection, so much patience? wherefore manifest such care of me? wherefore press me so earnestly? wherefore wait for me so long a while? Alas! a thousand times insulted by my sins, a thousand times irritated by my rebellions, He had only to let me lie stagnant in my sins, like so many others, or let me perish in them, as I have often thought would be the case. He would have done enough to show His mercy, and to satisfy His justice in my punishment. If He has wished to do more, if He has willed to preserve me, to wait for me, and to urge and press me in the way of salvation, it is only because, having chosen me by a particular grace, He wishes to finish the work that His mercy has commenced. "If the Lord had a mind to kill us," said the mother of Samson, "He would not have received a holocaust and libations at our hands" (Judges xiii. 23). I have a right to say the same as the mother of Samson, and to draw from the mercies that are past, an assurance of the mercies to come.

If God, irritated by my sins, had destined my destruction, would He have received the sacrifice of myself that I have made Him, and my entire consecration to His glory. It is without reserve and without division that I renew again to-day this universal sacrifice of myself; that I offer to Him this holocaust of charity. It is He Who has given me the thought and the courage to do this; it is He Who has given me the love which originated this thought, and is the principle of this courage; will it be more difficult for Him to crown that love by perseverance?

All those who read this Treatise may easily draw from it these pious sentiments, and therefore they may taste all the sweetness and the joy that they inspire, even though this moment may be for them the first moment of their conversion, and the first, too, of their consecration. Entering into the thoughts of the Apostle St. Paul, thoughts so consoling and so fit to comfort both penitents and the just, they may say to themselves for their consolation, " If God, irritated by our sins, had destined us to be the victims of His justice, would He have chosen us, among so many others, to load us with His blessings? would He have taken so many precautions to recall us from our sinful wanderings? would He have washed us so many times in the Blood of Jesus Christ?" No, without doubt. Thus it is certain that "God has not appointed us to wrath, but unto the purchasing of salvation by our Lord Jesus Christ" (1 Thess. v. 9); and in having given us a share in the Blood and in the merits of Jesus Christ, He has placed in our hands the price of this precious purchase, that is, of our salvation. What, then, can we desire more, since this infinite price is sufficient to purchase grace, to purchase perseverance, to purchase the crown of eternal glory!

It is thus that we should comfort ourselves in our distrusts. I venture to say, that those who would open their heart to all these reflections would find, as I have said, that their predestination, which was the subject of their alarm, would be, from this time, their great, their solid consolation. For if we are troubled by the fear that we are not of the number of the elect, on the contrary, to recognise by so many marks that we have reason to believe we are predestinated to eternal life, must give us the greatest consolation, gratitude, and joy.

Let us finish the proof of this truth, and draw from the temptation itself which I am combating a motive to comfort those whom it throws into trouble. In truth, whence comes this thought which so alarms you, O timorous and desolate souls! Is it grace which inspires you, or, rather, does it not come from the Evil one, the tempter? Certainly it is not grace; grace always inclines us to hope, to confide, to love. Is it, then, the demon who wishes to deceive you? How comes it that you are so credulous as to listen to this "father of lies?" But why does he make such great efforts to seduce you? it is because he knows the good will of Almighty God in your regard, and it is to render that good will ineffectual and without fruit, that he strives to discourage you, and even, if he can, to make you despair. Certainly, if you were abandoned by God, if you were the object of His vengeance and of His wrath, if the tempter knew it, he would not trouble you at all, nor strive to discourage you. Sure of having you in his net, he would only seek to amuse you by a deceitful calm. It is thus that he takes care, generally, not to disturb those who live in debauchery, and who are given to sensual indulgences. To such, he represents the mercy of God as always in their favour, and the way to Heaven as always easy. But whom does he endeavour to trouble, by suggesting to them terrifying ideas of the justice of God? They are those who confide holily in His mercy, and whose perfect conversion he fears. In their case, he does his utmost to exaggerate Almighty God's infinite justice and His anger, the difficulty of conversion, the rarity of perseverance, and the small number of the predestinate. He does this to lead them to abandon their practices of piety through discouragement, and, if he can, to cast them into despair. Let those whom he tempts in this way acknowledge the artifice of the demon, but let them acknowledge at the same time, in this temptation, the mercy of Almighty God in their regard, since it is only this abundant mercy that brings upon them the persecutions of this wicked spirit, who, seeing the happiness that awaits them, exerts his utmost malice to deprive them of it.

CHAPTER XXV.

WHO THOSE ARE WHO HAVE THE MOST CERTAIN MARKS OF PREDESTINATION. IT IS THEY WHO ARE IN AFFLICTION.

However pressing and conclusive these reflections may be, there are some Christians who have a greater right than others to deserve consolation from them, because they have a greater number of the particular marks of predestination. As it often happens that they do not give them sufficient attention, it is just that we now point them out. Who are they, then, who have these marks upon them of their predestination? It is they who are in sorrow, who are forgotten, who suffer dryness of spirit, who are in temptation, who have infirmities, who are in poverty, in disgrace, or in any other great or constant difficulty or affliction. It is a certain truth that the patient endurance of such sufferings is the true way of salvation. To suffer is the particular lot of souls chosen by God, and consequently the surest mark of predestination; so much so, that eternal salvation is as *easy* for those whom the world calls unhappy, as it is difficult for those who enjoy all worldly blessings. Shall I undertake to prove so certain a truth, so often repeated in the Holy Scripture ? "The world shall rejoice," said our Divine Lord to His disciples, "but you shall lament and weep" (St. John xvi. 20). It is true, that is, that your affliction shall be turned into joy, but you shall not taste the consolation there is in this joy till after you have felt the bitterness of affliction. "Blessed are they that mourn," said again Jesus Christ, "Blessed are they that weep," "Blessed are they who are persecuted, for theirs is the Kingdom of Heaven" (St. Matt. v. 5, etc.). Their right is acquired to the Heavenly inheritance, and they shall not be deprived of it. The lot of others is doubtful; there is always reason for them to fear, but for those who suffer, who weep, who are poor, who are persecuted, their predestination is, so to speak, evident, and the term or end of this predestination, which is Heaven, belongs to them already; God cannot deprive them of it without injustice. Why is that? It is because they are the true children of God, and it is to such children that the inheritance by right belongs.

But if the inheritance belongs to the children, it is for children to suffer the chastisements and corrections of their father. "My son," says the wise man, "when thou comest to the service of God, prepare thy soul for temptation, however afflicting that temptation or trial may be" (Ecclesiast. ii. 1). "Because thou wast acceptable to God," said the Angel to Tobias, "it was necessary that temptation should prove thee" (Tobias xii. 13). "Persevere under discipline," says St. Paul, writing to the Hebrews. "God dealeth with you as with His sons, for what son is there whom the father does not correct? But if you be without chastisement, whereof all" (that is, all God's true children) "are partakers, then are ye bastards, and not sons" (Heb. xii. 7, 8).

We must pass, then, through chastisement; that is, through afflictions and trials, to be assured that we are the true children of God. But if you are of the number of these true children, who are particularly cherished by God, can you doubt your predestination and your eternal salvation, since your suffering is the mark of it, provided that is, you bear it with patience, and resignation to the Holy Will of your Heavenly Father? An angel received an order from Almighty God to show to the Prophet Ezekiel who were the elect, the chosen ones, in the Holy City, who were not to be chastised in His indignation and fury. The Angel, to enable the Prophet to know who they were, marked each of them with the salutary sign of their predestination. This mark was a Hebrew letter—and it is worth while to observe, that, according to St. Jerome and other commentators, this letter was in the shape of a cross. But who are they who are honoured by this precious mark? Are they the kings, the great ones of the world, or the Priests of the Sanctuary, or the scrupulous observers of the law? No; the choice was not attached to any particular state or condition, it is attached only to suffering: "Mark Thau," (the Hebrew letter) "upon the foreheads of the men that *sigh and mourn* for all the abominations that are committed in the midst thereof" (Ezek. ix. 4). The letter Thau is the last letter of the Hebrew alphabet, and in the ancient Hebrew character had the form of a cross; it signifies also a sign or mark. Humility and patient suffering are, then, the surest marks of predestination.

This truth is still more clearly explained by another Prophet, the Prophet Zacharias (xiii. 8, 9). He divides the world under the figure of a holy people into three parts, and the third part, which is that of the elect, is characterised only by afflictions: "And there shall be in all the earth, saith the Lord, two parts in it which shall be scattered and shall perish, but the third part shall be left therein; and I will bring the third part through the fire, and will refine them as silver is refined, and I will try them as gold is tried. They shall call on My Name, and I will hear them. I will say thou art My people, and they shall say the Lord is my God." God disperses the two parts, He abandons them to their iniquity, and to their hardness of heart;

but He establishes, in the third part, the reign of His Mercy; He makes them His people, and He becomes their God.

But through what treatment did God, Who is goodness itself, make them pass? " I will make them pass through the fire, and will refine them as silver is refined, and I will try them as gold is tried." It is thus that Almighty God treats His own beloved children, who are predestinated to the glory of Heaven. He does not spare them. He subjects some to the pains of sickness, others to the trials of continual scruples, others to the malignity of evil tongues, others to the rigours of penance, others to a cruel martyrdom. He makes them pass through the fire, not like wood to be consumed, but like gold to be refined, and destined for some excellent work, and has therefore to be put into the crucible. The gold seems in this state to suffer, as it were, and to be marred; it melts and becomes soft, it loses its force and its brightness, till at length the time comes to take it out of the fire; and when it comes from the crucible, it is, for its exceeding beauty, the astonishment and admiration of all who behold it. It has become a precious and magnificent vase, of which the matter is all pure, and the work of a marvellous beauty. Such is the destiny of the elect. It is not only expedient for them to suffer, but it is their state and their portion. To suffer, therefore, or, as the Scripture expresses it, to pass through the fire, is a precious mark of predestination; and the more bitter is the suffering, the more the faithful soul should recognise in that bitterness the solid foundations of its confidence. "Let us believe," said the heroic Judith to the people, in their affliction, "that these scourges of our Lord have happened for our amendment, and not for our destruction" (Judith viii. 27).

Let us examine more profoundly this truth, so capable of confounding the happy ones of the world, who seek to taste every pleasure, but so consoling to those who open their eyes only to see, like Job, their continual losses, who experience in outward things nothing but misfortune, and within only bitterness and sadness. Ah! how often it happens that they do not know their happiness; they call their trials and afflictions misfortunes—scourges of Almighty God, and marks of His anger—whilst they are in truth the standard marks of His mercy, since they are the marks of their predestination.

CHAPTER XXVI.

PROOFS OF THE PRECEDING TRUTHS. FIRST, IT IS IN SUFFERINGS THAT WE FIND THE TRUEST VOCATIONS.

I WOULD ask what is the best means of securing our salvation? What is it that makes Saints and the predestinate? It is first, as I have said, the vocation of God; it is the expiation of past sins, it is the precaution against relapses, and which includes all the rest, it is likeness to Jesus Christ. It does not want, assuredly, anything more to make a Saint, or to recognise one of the predestinated. Now, where are we to seek for all these advantages? In sufferings. It is there you will find them all. It is there, then, that you will find the assurance of a blessed predestination.

First, we find there the vocation of God. It is true, God calls all Christians. "Wisdom," saith the Scripture, "preacheth abroad; she uttereth her voice in the streets" (Prov. i. 20); she invites all the world to come to hear, but the greater number, allured by their worldly pursuits, do not listen to her voice. The Father of the family, in the Gospel, invites all his neighbours to the nuptials of His Son; but no one who is invited is willing to come. One is rich and is occupied with his property; another thinks of becoming so, and is making his purchases; a third is absorbed with the pleasures of this life. All have their excuses, so that no one profits by the nuptial feast which has been prepared for them. The Father of the family, irritated by their indifference, by their negligence, or their contempt, leaves them to their worldly occupations, which constitute their happiness and their end. He transfers the favour, which He would have shown them, to the poor, to the infirm, to the miserable, who are the objects of the world's contempt. It is they who partake of the feast; but how do they get to it? A kind of violence is done them, "and they are compelled to enter the nuptial guest-chamber.

They are pressed, they are, if I may say so, pushed in, they are forced to enter. Of what is this compulsion a figure? It is affliction, which detaches us in spite of ourselves, as it were, by a holy violence, from the world that we love, and obliges us to accept the invitations of our good God; those invitations we despised, whilst enjoying the pleasures of the world. Thus, the Son of God, wishing to prepare us for this application of the parable, has added to it as its conclusion—"Many are called, but few are chosen" (St. Matt. xxii. 14); as if He said, It is true that there are few chosen, and that many are called; but you see who are the one and who are the other. The happy ones of the world are called, and they are not chosen; but the unhappy ones, in the world's estimation, and the poor and the suffering are chosen, among the number of the elect. It is this which instructs us as to the two different means which Almighty God employs to attract us to Himself. He invites some with sweetness; there are others whom He presses and prostrates, like St. Paul, whom He puts in chains, whom He obliges, by a sort of violence, to give themselves to Him. This violence, however, does not fall upon the will, for the will is always free; but it falls on what surrounds the will, I mean, on the objects of its attachments which God takes away from it with violence, to oblige it, to compel it to detach itself from them. Now it is easy to see which of these two methods is the most powerful, and therefore the most efficacious. We know, alas, that there are very few who yield themselves up to the sweet attractions of grace; and for one who sacrifices with a good heart the advantages of this life, which he might enjoy at will, there are a thousand who do not make this sacrifice, but by dint of afflictions. Again, how long does a rebellious heart hold out in combat with Almighty God! It leans as long as it can upon all its surroundings, it exhausts all human resources before coming to the point of laying down its arms, and owning itself conquered. We do as the passengers did in the ship which carried the Prophet Jonas; when they found themselves in danger of perishing with him, "each one called upon his god," the god that he knew, the god that he adored, the god that he loved. Thus we act, when God sends us afflictions, in order to lead us to Himself. There are gods whom our heart adores, and to whom it has recourse; these gods are riches, the fortune of relations, our patrons, our own ability, on which we always count. These are the gods in whom we place our principal confidence, and to whom we say "deliver us, save us." But these gods have no power—we soon find their weakness—and when we are plunged in a sea of bitterness, from which no human help can draw us, we then have recourse to God, we call upon Him, we recognise His justice, we submit to His Will; we are, as it were, forced to take this part, because there is no other means to console us in our trouble.

How many are there who will acknowledge, in their own experience, the truth of what I have now stated, and who will confess with sincerity and justice, that if God had not detached them from the world by afflictions, if He had not imparted a salutary bitterness to the objects of their passions, if He had not sown thorns on the path of their ambition, or of their pleasures, to disgust them, they would have preserved even to the end the criminal attachments by which they were enchained! How many have commenced to live a Christian life, only when they began to be afflicted; who did not open their eyes to the truths of the Catholic faith till they were open to the misfortunes which befell them, and who would not have wept penitential tears unless they had shed them first over their losses, their afflictions, and their infirmities. How many without the disgrace into which they fell, with some powerful patron or benefactor, without the loss of their property, or without some other great calamity, would never have dreamed of entertaining the true sentiments of Christian humility! Amused by a vain phantom of devotion, they nourished their self-love with all the appearances of good works, in which they gloried; they thought that they were just and faithful, and applauded themselves for their pretended sanctity; yet they were further away from God by their pride than others would have been by their crimes. The hour of their conversion came, and that of salvation. God made them hear efficaciously His voice, and how? They were humbled by some signal disgrace, and humility, which is so necessary for salvation, entered their heart by the door of humiliation.

How many others are there whom God treats in the same way, and who would have passed all their days in pleasure, in joy, and in plenty if God had not recalled them to Himself, by snatching from their hands the objects of their attachments. To one He sends a painful and dangerous sickness, to another the loss of his property. With one it is the ruin of his health—he cannot go any more into company, which had been to him a snare, a temptation, and an occasion of sin. With another it is the loss of his patron and protector, and all his hopes are buried with him. Another discredited in his business, by the misfortunes of the time, is constrained to quit it. Sometimes death takes away relations and friends—a husband, or children—they cannot find consolation on this earth. There is no one but Almighty God Who comes Himself to this afflicted heart, to offer it a solid consolation in

His love. At length He is recognised as the true friend, the friend at all times, the friend who continues always. Behold what passes every day; and perhaps the reader knows it by his own experience. This is what I mean by an efficacious vocation, because it has almost always its effect; it is this vocation which is the first step to be taken on the road to predestination, and which is its first mark.

CHAPTER XXVII.

SECOND PROOF. IT IS IN SUFFERING THAT WE FIND THE SUREST EXPIATION OF SIN. ADVANTAGES OF INVOLUNTARY AFFLICTIONS ABOVE VOLUNTARY PENANCES.

WHAT I have said of vocation, I may say also of the expiation of sin, and of the precaution not to commit it again. Both the one and the other, which we know are essentially necessary for salvation, are found, generally, in afflictions and in sufferings.

With regard to the expiation of sin, who is there, that without the involuntary misfortunes of life, its sicknesses, its accidents, its annoyances, its contradictions, its sufferings, and its losses, would dream of expiating so many sins of his past life, and so many daily faults, which we commit every moment? We know, however, that there is no salvation without penance, and we cannot bring ourselves to do it, or if we do it, it is so little, and so mild, that it cannot be of much merit.

In this state of things we would wish to spend our life, and for not having done penance we might find ourselves, perhaps, condemned hereafter to do eternally in hell the fruitless penance of the devils, if a merciful God did not Himself prepare the means to exact from us the satisfaction His justice demands, but which our laxity refuses to give Him.

It is this thought which should comfort those who, when in affliction, fear that the penance it imposes upon them is not agreeable to God, and therefore is not an expiation for their sins, because it is involuntary. This is an error. I can assure them that the pains which God imposes are as fit to satisfy for their sins as the most austere maceration of the flesh which they could give themselves of their own choice. I think that they are, in a certain sense, even more fit to appease the justice of God, than any private and self-chosen mortifications, however great. For, first of all, these involuntary afflictions come clearly from Almighty God; they are the Will of God in our regard, since nothing can happen to us without the salutary disposition of His Providence, a character which voluntary mortifications rarely have, for they are often regulated by caprice, or self-love, or self-will.

Secondly, they are often more rigorous and painful, and therefore more satisfactory for our sins. For what comparison is there between the fasts, the disciplines, or the hair-shirt of a solitary, and the lively pains of an obstinate sickness, the perpetual contradiction of a wayward husband, or of a cross wife, or of a master whose whims must be borne with every moment, the extremities to which great poverty reduces us, or the trouble and the humiliation which are brought on, by the loss of reputation or of fortune!

Thirdly, these involuntary sufferings are

CHAPTER XXVIII.

THIRD PROOF. IN AFFLICTIONS WE FIND THE MOST CERTAIN MEANS OF AVOIDING SIN FOR THE FUTURE.

WHAT is the most usual source of sin? It is abundance and pleasure, power and glory. It is thus that are engendered sensuality, vanity, malignity, the contempt of others, the forgetfulness of God, and often the utter loss of the Faith. What surer means of guarding against these evils than afflictions? There are two obvious reasons for this — the one is that afflictions teach us to fear the Justice and Power of Him Who overthrows, when He wishes, all our projects, our might and our pride, and Who avenges, sooner or later, the contempt of His law. The other is, that the natural effect of the salutary losses and afflictions which God sends us, is to separate us from the objects of our attachments, and thus to purify the heart.

For the truth of what I am saying, I call to witness those who may read this Treatise, and who, perhaps, are in that state of affliction and trial of which I am praising the advantages. If they are just to themselves, they will acknowledge that they have begun to leave off a life of sin when Almighty God had laid His Hand heavy upon them to remove from them the occasions of sin, and to break in pieces those earthly idols which shared the worship of their heart; so that if He had restored to them the property or the pleasures of which He had deprived them, they would, in all probability, have given themselves up again to the same passions as before, because they would have the same facilities as before of gratifying them.

You are troubled because your infirmities continue always the same. By the use of remedies you lengthen out a languishing life. You have become useless to the world, and you are no longer sought by society. If you had good health, you would be able to enjoy, as formerly, all the pleasures of the neighbourhood, and of the city. Balls, theatres, games, and society would welcome you again as heretofore. You would again lose your time in these baneful amusements. The world would not do without you, and you would not do without the world. The charms of your society would captivate afresh the hearts of your worshippers, and they would again carry you away with them to work iniquity. What would you gain, then, by the recovery of your health? You are sad, because fortune, so favourable to others, has for you only refusals. Alas! if it again smiled upon you as upon them, it would elate you as it elates them—like them you would soon forget, in your elevation of mind, a God whom pride disowns, and Who is only truly served by the humble. You would become again high-minded and proud. What would you gain by the change? Would it be for the better or for the worse? You would become again full of disdain, and contempt of others, unjust in your pretensions and in your vengeance, and negligent in your duties.

You are, then, annoyed because you live in poverty; but if you were rich, would you be more holy? would you not be, on the contrary, more sensual and more vain in your expenses since you do not desire the health you have not, except to procure those vanities and conveniences, and those pleasures from which poverty excludes you? It is, then, for you an advantage to be infirm, to be weak, to be poor, to have lost your fortune, since these misfortunes have drawn you from a state which is for so many the approximate occasion of sin, and such it has been to you in former days.

Now what surer mark of the merciful design that God has had to save you from the common ruin, than for Him to remove from you all dangerous occasions? Can you doubt, after this, that He wishes to count you among the number of those whom He has chosen for Heaven? Is it not thus that He acts towards those whose obduracy obliges Him to treat as reprobates? He lets them live on according to their own desires, and, as St. Cyprian says, He leaves these unhappy victims of His eternal anger to get fat at leisure on the riches of the world, that He might immolate them hereafter with more glory to His justice; but for those whom He has predestinated, He does not suffer them to turn aside from the way of salvation without punishing them; and if they have turned aside from it, He leads them back by afflictions. It is thus that He has treated all those who have been, before you, the object of His most precious favours. If He treats you in this manner, it is a sign that He cherishes you as He has cherished them, and that He wishes, by the same trials, to conduct you to the same unfading crowns.

CHAPTER XXIX.

FOURTH AND LAST PROOF. AFFLICTIONS FORM IN US THE LIKENESS TO JESUS CHRIST. THIS LIKENESS IS THE CONSUMMATION OF PREDESTINATION.

LET us consider the proof of this truth, by the last mark of predestination, or rather its only mark, since it includes all the rest. We shall find this beautiful mark in those whom God afflicts. What is it? I have already stated it; and we know it well enough. It is likeness to Jesus Christ. "Those whom God foreknew," saith the Apostle, "He also predestinated to be made conformable to the image of His Son" (Rom. viii. 29). Jesus Christ, while on earth, was a man of sorrows, Who experienced all our miseries, and Who was satiated with humiliations. God created man, saith Tertullian, in the image of His Son. He had, then, in His idea, the nature that His Son should take when He should come down upon the earth; and He wished that His Son should be the model after which He created the first man. Such was the thought of this Father. Be that as it may at any rate, we may affirm that Almighty God had most assuredly the same design in the sanctification of man, of which the sanctity of Jesus Christ is the model; so that if man is destined to share in Heaven the glory of the Son of God, he is destined also to share, while on earth, in His sufferings. "If we suffer we shall also reign with Him," saith St. Paul (2 Tim. ii. 12). We are obliged, then, to carry our cross with Him, to carry it as He carried it, and to finish our sacrifice upon it, in union with our Lord's death upon the Cross. This He expects of His fidelity. This "is to be faithful unto death." "If any man will come after Me, let him deny himself, and take up his cross daily and follow Me" (Luke ix. 20).

Follow Me where? to Calvary, to die upon the Cross.

I do not stop to prove the indispensable necessity which is imposed upon us to fulfil this obligation, and to form in us this holy conformity. We are all well aware of this great truth; but I should wish that we felt more the consolation that it ought to produce in the hearts of those in whom misfortunes and poverty, sufferings and persecutions have commenced to form so happy a resemblance to Jesus Christ. Since, then, conformity to Jesus Christ has a strict and close connection with predestination, and there can be no predestination without this conformity, what ought we to think when Almighty God takes Himself the care, by means of salutary afflictions, to make us like to His Son, and to conform us to His image? What, I say, ought to be our thoughts, when He makes us to drink of His chalice of bitterness, which His well-beloved Son drank to the very dregs, and which He nailed, so to speak, with Him to His Cross? Ought we to resist, put ourselves in trouble, and to complain? complain that we are destined to share the glory of the Son of God in Heaven! No, doubtless; but ought we to disquiet ourselves about our salvation and predestination? ought we to listen to the tempter when he suggests that mercy is not for us? No! we have only to let ourselves be conducted by our good God, and to conform ourselves to His all-holy, and all-wise, and all-perfect Will. We have only to let God act, and to repose in Him. Since He has begun in us this conformity to the image—the crucified Image of His Divine Son—we have only to let Him finish this great and glorious work, and wait on Him in patience and in hope. What consolation to be made like to Jesus Christ! Surely we should cry out with the Royal Prophet, "Thy rod and Thy staff have comforted me;" the rod of Thy justice, and the staff of Thy anger, in chastising me, have been my consolation.

Let the people of the world be saddened, O my good God, with Your chastisements; let them desire to turn them aside; let them seek in creatures, and in worldly amusement, their frivolous consolations; let them address to You their prayers to obtain deliverance from these salutary trials. For myself, I have but one prayer to offer You, and but one only desire—I wish to carry the amiable Cross of my Saviour, to carry it with Him, to be attached to it with Him, to die on it with Him. This Cross, in which I desire to glory, and in nothing else, shall take the place of every other joy; and when all the consolations of the earth shall have abandoned me, it will be itself my great consolation. With it I shall not fear either temptations or the tempter, nor all hell armed to destroy me. Possessing this precious pledge of my predestination, I shall not yield any more to timid alarms, and placing in this treasure all my confidence, sufferings shall henceforth be in my sight the consoling marks of Your favour, and the way in which I hope to endure them, will be, in Your Eyes, a most convincing proof of my love.

CHAPTER XXX.

RECAPITULATION OR ABRIDGMENT OF ALL THAT IS CONTAINED IN THIS WORK.

I HOPE that all that are in affliction, of whatever kind it may be, will find in this Treatise wherewith to console them in their trials, and to sweeten their bitterness. I hope, also, that those whom excessive fear has cast into trouble and dejection will find in the reflections of this Treatise wherewith to calm all their alarms. It is in their favour that I think I ought to make, before concluding it, an abstract or summary of all that it contains, in order that they who read it, may see at a glance the number and the strength of the proofs I have employed, the order and the suitableness of the replies I have made to the suggestions of the tempter, so that their united force may make on their minds a stronger impression.

Though there is a salutary fear which ought never to leave the hearts of the just, there is an excessive fear, the effects of which on the soul are serious, if not fatal. These effects are discouragement and sadness, but principally the weakening in the tenderness of the love we ought to have for God. This tenderness God expects of us, and of which He furnishes us the model, in the tenderness with which He loves us Himself. But the timorous and distrustful know nothing of it; it is only found in those who have a lively confidence in the goodness of their Saviour. It is this holy confidence which I am so anxious to be the means of imparting to the hearts of all the faithful.

Nothing can be more solid than this confidence, since it is founded on the promises of God, and on His truthfulness and fidelity, and what is still more apt to excite it in us, on a goodness and mercy so incomprehensible, that the multitude of our sins has not discouraged it, nor the number of His infinite blessings has not exhausted it.

But if this confidence is solid, it appears no less indispensable; the advantages we derive from it would suffice to oblige us to yield ourselves to its sweet embrace, since it honours God in a manner, the most noble and glorious, and in it we find the joy and repose of the heart, the fervour of charity, strength in temptation, consolation in trial, and therefore a powerful aid to our salvation. In vain do the over timid allow themselves to be affrighted by the severity of God's judgments, since Jesus, the God of goodness, is far more amiable than He is terrible; and to favour us, and, as it were, to prove His tenderness in our regard, He has remitted our final judgment into the Hands of Jesus Christ, His Son, become man for the love of us, and therefore full of goodness and compassion for us, by reason of His Divine Humanity. This compassion our Divine Lord has evidenced by the titles He has taken, of our Brother, our Spouse, and our Friend, and by His experience as Jesus Christ, the God-Man, of our infirmities and our weaknesses. How is it possible, then, not to count on a favourable judgment from a Judge so compassionate for His brethren, so tender towards His friends, and Who seems more interested for His Own glory, than even by His tenderness for us, that that judgment should acquit us? But how can we be alarmed when this compassionate Judge condescends to be at the same time our advocate as well as intercessor, and to supply our want of merit by covering our misery with His own infinite merits, and to give us, by means of His Precious Blood, a claim and right to exact from God, His Father, by a kind of justice, the mercy we hope for?

If the timid soul would nourish her distrust by the sight of her own sins and imperfections, she finds even here a ground of comfort when she sees how good God is, not only to the just, but particularly to sinners, since He loves them sinners as they are, and since He regards them not only with compassion, but with tenderness; for He calls them, He seeks them, He waits for them, He receives them, as the father of the family received his prodigal son in the Gospel, without exacting any other price for their pardon (which He grants without delay) than their sorrow, their confidence, and their love, and that He creates those dispositions within them; and lastly, that even in His reproaches, His chastisements, and His menaces, all is tender and amiable in this God of goodness.

How much, then, is there which ought to calm the distrusts of the timid and fearful, and that might well open their hearts to the sweet sentiments of a tender confidence in our Saviour. There is but one subject left that affrights them, it is the small number of the elect. But there is comfort still even in a truth in itself so terrifying. There is great comfort for the just, and for those who have reason to believe that they belong to this small and happy number. They can find in themselves, in their history, the marks of their predestination; they see that God full of mercy in their regard, has favoured them with many particular and personal graces and gifts which He bestows only on those for whom He has a singular love, and also that He conducts them by the same road as those of His elect whom he has already crowned.

Such souls, then, whether just or penitent, may recognize in themselves these marks; the tempter does his utmost, however, to trouble them by unreasonable fears, either to retain them in the chains of sin, or to make them return to it. But the afflicted may recognize these marks more clearly still whom God has made partakers of the Cross of His Son, who pass their life in suffering, from whatever quarter it may come, and of what kind soever it may be; for such, their predestination is not only probable, but it seems almost certain, since they find in this state of suffering the vocation the most efficacious, the expiation of their past sins the most entire, and an infallible precaution against sin for the future, and therefore such have the true marks upon them of final predestination.

CHAPTER XXXI.

CONCLUSION OF THE TREATISE. WE CONFIDE IN GOD FOR TEMPORAL THINGS, WE MUST CONFIDE IN HIM ALSO FOR OUR SALVATION AND OUR PREDESTINATION.

LET us conclude this Treatise by a reflection, which, while it confirms all that we have said on the marks of predestination, confirms also all that we have established as to the effect which the mercy of God should produce in us.

We are all well enough agreed that we must trust in the providence of God for our temporal wants: for our health, our property, and life. This confidence should banish the trouble and the disquietude which are often felt by those who are attached to the goods of this world; and though we ought not to tempt God, nor abandon, under the pretext of confidence, the care of our temporal affairs; we know, notwithstanding, that we ought to lean upon this universal Providence, Who takes care of all who trust in it. "Cast thy care upon the Lord," saith the Royal Prophet, "and He shall sustain thee" (Ps. liv. 33). We acknowledge that the more peaceable is this confidence, the purer is our Christianity, and the more perfect is our virtue. Why, then, should we not put our whole confidence in God in the great affair of our salvation? Is it that Almighty God has less anxiety to save us than to feed us? and shall we pardon on this subject those distrusts which we do not venture to allow in our temporal necessities? It is true, that the whole earth is His, and He holds in His hands all our wealth, that He is master of our health and of our life. He is, as Holy Scripture tells us, the Lord of life and of death. But is He not also called the "God of salvation," the "God of my salvation?" (Ps. xxxvii. 23); that is to say, the God Who desires our salvation, Who labours for our salvavation. Why, then, should we not say of our eternal salvation (in which I venture to remark that God interests Himself more than we do), what we should say with confidence of the temporal aid we expect at His hands?

"The Lord ruleth me, and I shall want nothing;

"He hath set me in a place of pasture.

"He hath brought me up on the waters of refreshment.

"He hath converted my soul.

"He hath set me in the paths of justice for His own Name's sake.

"For though I should walk in the midst of the shadow of death, I will fear no evils, for Thou art with me.

"Thy rod and Thy staff, they have comforted me.

"Thou hast prepared a table for me against them that afflict me.

"Thou hast anointed my head with oil, and my chalice, which inebriates me, how good is it!

"And Thy mercy will follow me all the days of my life,

"And that I may dwell in the House of the Lord unto length of days" (Psalm xxii.).

APPENDIX.

CONFIDENCE IN GOD:

A PRAYER OF ST. GERTRUDE AND ST. MECHTILDE.

(Taken from "The Prayers of St. Gertrude and St. Mechtilde.")

OUR LORD said to St. Mechtilde: Of a truth it greatly pleases Me that men should confidently expect great things from Me, for it is impossible that a man should fail to obtain that which he believes and hopes for. Therefore it is good to hope great things from Me, and to confide sincerely in Me. Our Lord gave also a like assurance to St. Gertrude.

PRAYER.

O GOD of my heart, my only hope and refuge, I, the poorest of Thy creatures, and infinitely unworthy of the least good at Thy hands, do yet so confidently hope in Thy tender kindness, that I have no manner of doubt that as Thou knowest how to succour and to aid me, so Thou both canst and wilt be with me in all things. I know, indeed, O compassionate God, that if Thou wert to deal with me as I have deserved, I could expect no grace at Thy hand, but only manifold rebuke and punishment: but since I know that Thy goodness is so exuberant that Thou art wont to do good, even to Thy worst enemies, I most firmly believe and trust that Thou wilt not forsake me in my distress and miseries, but wilt provide for me with a care and generosity which I should vainly look for in my dearest friend. Most loving God, although my sins are so manifold and so grievous that they deserve a thousand hells, yet by reason of Thy infinite goodness, I so sincerely expect from Thee remission of them all, provided only they grieve me, as in deed and in truth they do, that I could more easily doubt my own existence than the certainty of this remission. O Infinite Goodness, so tender is my confidence in Thee, that even if I had sinned a thousand times more than I have, and knew that Thine anger was fiercely kindled against me, yet, could I choose my own judge, I would choose none other than Thee. In Thee alone, and in none other than Thee, could I trust, and I should more certainly hope for mercy at Thy hand, than from my best and dearest friend. For if I had sinned as often and as grievously against any one of my friends, as I have against Thee, I am most sure that I could not hope for pardon even from the most tender and compassionate of mothers. Yea, had I been so rebellious and so unloving to my own mother, as I have been to Thee, she would have cast me off for ever. But Thou, notwithstanding the many and grievous insults I have heaped upon Thee, and notwithstanding all my many and grievous negligences in Thy service, dost still cherish and sustain me. And dost Thou think, O most loving Father, that I have the smallest doubt that I shall attain to everlasting bliss? do Thou Thyself forbid. For my hope of attaining that bliss rests not on my own merits, but on the faithful promise of Thy only-begotten Son, and on His most abundant and exuberant merits, which He has communicated and made over to His elect. And hence I abound with such great joy and consolation, because I seem already to possess that for which I so eagerly long. For Thy Son, Who has promised me salvation and His merits, which are its title and its price, is most faithful, nor can any word which has gone forth from His mouth be revoked or fail. Vouchsafe, O Eternal Father, to increase in me this hope and trust, which I give into Thy merciful keeping, until I see Thee in Thy unfading eternity, and hope be lost in fruition. Amen.

FROM THE SPIRITUAL CONQUEST.—P. 423.

"THAT CONFIDENCE IN GOD'S GOODNESS IS THE MAIN SUPPORT OF OUR SPIRITUAL EDIFICE.

"We must be confident that our loving Lord will, first, pardon our sins; secondly, strengthen us in all our necessities; thirdly, bring us, finally, to eternal happiness. And to strengthen this confidence, we must deeply engrave these two following maxims in our souls, and then we shall easily be content to leave ourselves in the arms of His paternal Providence, and lose ourselves in the abyss of His piety: First, that whatever befalls us, comes immediately from His Will or His permission. Secondly, that He will turn all, even our frailties and failings, to our spiritual good. We may further weigh what wonderful cause we have for confidence and comfort.

"I. First, in heaven, where we have : *Bowels of Mercy*, in God the Father, to Whom we cry daily as His Son taught us: 'Our Father, Who art in heaven.' Will not a good father forgive the fault and forget the folly of his returning and repentant child?

"II. *Wounds of Mercy* in God the Son, the least of which was sufficient to redeem a thousand worlds: whereby we, being reconciled and made His friends, will He deny us anything which is necessary? Is not each drop of His dear Blood a motive of loving confidence, and able to melt us into a filial dependency on Him?

"III. *Promises of Mercy* in God the Holy Ghost, Who hath assured us of His continual comforts till the consummation of the world.

"IV. *Words of Mercy*, when He said : '*As I live, I desire not the death of the wicked, but that the wicked turn from his way and live. Turn ye, turn ye, from your evil ways, and why will you die, O House of Israel.*' What hard heart would not be touched with tenderness, and say reciprocally : 'As I live, O my Lord God, I detest all sin, and convert myself totally to Thee, that I may live with Thee, and love Thee eternally.' O holy conversion! O happy contract!

"V. *Breasts of Mercy* in the Mother of Jesus. O Jesus, be to us a Jesus! O Mother of Jesus, be to us a Mother of mercies! let the care of our honour be ever in our hearts, and the care of our welfare always in them!

"VI. *Castles of Mercy* in the angels, who are before and behind us, to watch over and protect us.

"VII. *Oracles of Mercy*, the prayers and sufferings of all the saints; pitying our misery, and purchasing salvation for us. If we put this all together, we shall find all heaven for us. What matter, then, if all hell be against us? *Why are ye fearful, O ye of little faith?*

"Secondly, on earth in the Church Militant, what is not for us? Sacraments, Scriptures, Examples, Prayers. If we go not to heaven, in whom lies the fault? What could God do, that He hath not done? and what could we have more than we have for our consolation and salvation? Who can but take courage, comfort, and confidence?

"Thirdly, look upon Christ Jesus. Why came He into this world? How did He conduct Himself in it towards sinners both in His life and death? Why was He called Jesus, and termed a friend of publicans and sinners? Why did He say that He came to call sinners and not the just, and to do mercy and not justice? What access and comfort gave He to all sinners? What was His last will and testament? What His last words? '*Father, forgive them, for they know not what they do!*'

"Fourthly, ponder God's perfections. He is our Maker, we the work of His hands! Doth not every artist love his own handiwork? Hath not every one a natural proneness to protect, improve, profit, and perfect his own? Even so, our loving Lord taketh care of us! He hides and harbours us, as *the hen doth gather her chickens under her wings.* He defends us, *as the apple of His eye. Can a woman forget her infant, so as not to have pity on the son of her womb,* and '*if she should forget,*' says our Lord, '*yet will I not forget thee, because, I have graven thee on My hands.*' He is all might, all wisdom, all goodness'; put these together: I have a Father and Maker that loves me exceedingly; He knows my necessities, and what is best for me; He is rich enough to provide for me. Will He let me perish? Will He reject me? Then reason further with yourself, thus, 'In whom shall I confide, if not in God? in myself or in others? We are all inconstant; all ignorant of what is best; all impotent, and require means to help us. *It is good to confide in the Lord,* rather than *to have confidence in man.*'

"Fifthly, reflect upon our own experience. Whom did God ever deceive in His promises? Who ever heartily called upon Him, and was refused? Hath He not hitherto marvellously protected and preserved you, and disposed all for your good? Why, then, should you doubt or distrust His Providence for the time to come? No: *Blessed be the man that trusteth in the Lord. Heaven and earth shall pass away,* but no tittle of my hope in Thee, my dear and only Saviour. This shall be my anchor and stay: *although*

He shall kill me, I will trust in Him. I will rest secure in His Divine Providence, and endeavour to get an habitual and stable trust in His paternal protection, without any care or fear, as doth a child in his mother's bosom. This is the ready way to become immovable and immutable, quiet and contented.

"Is He God? Is He good? Is He my God, my Father, my Jesus, Jesus crucified? Is His goodness infinite? Doth He want power, wisdom, or will, to pardon, protect and perfect me? I must surely have little faith, less hope, and no love, if I will not take Thy words, O Lord, Thy works, Thy wounds, Thy life, and Thy love as secure pledges of Thy care towards me, and as sufficient motives to place my whole confidence in Thee."

THE END.

PATERNOSTER ROW NO. 18, LONDON.

R. WASHBOURNE'S CATALOGUE.

FEBRUARY, 1876.

The Sufferings of our Lord Jesus Christ. Preached in London by Father Claude de la Colombière, S. J., in the Chapel Royal, St. James's, in the year 1677. 18mo. 1s. ; red edges, 1s. 6d.

Lenten Thoughts. Drawn from the Gospel for each day in Lent. By the Bishop of Northampton 1s. 6d. ; stronger bound, 2s. ; red edges, 2s. 6d.

Devotions for Public and Private Use at the Way of the Cross. By Sister M. F. Clare (the Nun of Kenmare). Illustrated with the Pictures of the Stations. 16mo. 1s. ; red edges, 1s. 6d.

The Continental Fish Cook; or, a Few Hints on Maigre Dinners. By M. J. N. de Frederic. 18mo. 1s.

A Treatise on Confidence in the Mercy of God. By Mgr. Languet. Translated by Abbot Burder.

Sanctuary Meditations for Priests and Frequent Communicants. Translated from the Spanish.

Letters to my God-Child — Letter IV. On the Veneration of the Blessed Virgin. By Mrs. Stuart Laidlaw. 16mo. 4d.

Bessy; or the Fatal Consequence of Telling Lies. By the writer of "The Rat Pond, or the Effects of Disobedience." 1s. ; cloth gilt, 1s. 6d.

The Serving Boy's Manual and Book of Public Devotions, containing all those prayers and devotions for Sundays and Holidays, usually divided in their recitation between the Priest and the

---

*** *Though this Catalogue does not contain many of the books of other Publishers, R. W. can supply all of them, no matter by whom they are published.*

Congregation. Compiled from approved sources, and adapted to Churches, served either by the Secular or the Regular Clergy.

IN THE PRESS.

Stories for my Children.—The Angels and the Sacraments. Square 16mo. 1s. ; extra cloth, 2s. 6d.

Semi-Tropical Trifles. By Herbert Compton. Fcp. 8vo. Fancy boards, 1s.

Lives of the First Religious of the Visitation of Holy Mary. By Mother Frances Magdalen de Chaugy. With two Photographs. 2 vols., cr. 8vo. 12s.

Easy Way to God. By Cardinal Bona. Translated by Father Collins, author of "Cistercian Legends," "Spiritual Conferences." Fcap. 8vo. 3s.

Legends of the Saints. By M. F. S., author of "Stories of the Saints." Square 16mo.

Spiritual Conferences on the Mysteries of Faith and the Interior Life. By Father Collins, author of "Cistercian Legends," &c. Cr. 8vo. 4s.

Lives of the Saints for every Day in the Year. Translated from M. Didot's edition. Beautifully printed on thick toned paper, with borders from ancient sources, scarlet cloth gilt, gilt edges, 4to. 16s.

The Mass : and a devout method of assisting at it. From the French of M. Tronson. 4d.

Canon Schmid's Tales, selected from his works. New translation, with Original Illustrations, 3s. 6d. Separately: Canary Bird, 6d.; Dove, 6d.; Inundation, 6d. Rose Tree, 6d.; Water Jug, 6d. ; Wooden Cross, 6d.

The Elements of Gregorian or Plain Chant and Modern Music. By the Professor of Music and Organist in All Hallows' College, Dublin. 2s. 6d.

The English Religion. Letters addressed to an Irish Gentleman. By A. M. 1s.

Confraternity of the Holy Family. By Henry Edward, Cardinal-Archbishop of Westminster. 8vo. 3d.

Elevations to the Heart of Jesus. By Rev. Father Doyotte, S. J. Fcap. 8vo. 3s.

S. Vincent Ferrer, of the Order of Friar Preachers: his Life, Spiritual Teaching, and practical Devotion. By the Rev. Fr. Andrew Pradel, of the same Order. Translated from the French by the Rev. Fr. T. A. Dixon, O.P. With a Photograph. Crown 8vo. 5s.

The History of the Italian Revolution. The Revolution of the Barricades. (1796—1849.) By the Chevalier O'Clery, M.P., K.S.G. 8vo. 7s. 6d.

Stories of Holy Lives. By M. F. S., author of "Stories of the Saints," "Catherine Hamilton," "Catherine grown Older," "Tom's Crucifix and other Tales." Fcp. 8vo. 3s.

The Rule of our most holy Father St. Benedict, Patriarch of Monks. From the old English edition of 1638. Edited by one of the Benedictine Fathers of St. Michael's, near Hereford. Fcap. 8vo. 4s. 6d.

First Communion Picture. Tastefully printed in gold and colours. Price 1s., or 10s. a dozen, *net*.

"Just what has long been wanted, a really good picture, with Tablet for First Communion and Confirmation."—*Tablet*.

Book of Family Crests and Mottos. Upwards of four thousand engravings. Eleventh edition. 2 vols., cr. 8vo., 24s.

New Testament, Catholic Vers., Notes and References, 19 large Illustrations. Large 4to., cloth gilt, 12s. 6d.

Road to Heaven. A game for family parties. By Miss M. A. Macdaniel. 3s. 6d.

Balmes' Letters to a Sceptic on Matters of Religion. 6s.

The Dove of the Tabernacle. By Fr. Kinane. 1s. 6d.

Munster Firesides; or, the Barrys of Beigh. By E. Hall. 3s. 6d.

The Mirror of Faith: your Likeness in it. By Father Cuthbert. 3s.

The Christian Instructed in the Nature and Use of Indulgences. By Rev. F. A. Maurel. 3s.

New Model for Youth; or, Life of Richard Aloysius Pennefather. 3s. 6d.

The Blessed Sacrament of the Miracle. 10 Photographs. Price 2s. 6d.

Recollections of Cardinal Wiseman, &c. By M. J. Arnold. 2s. 6d.

The Child. By Mgr. Dupanloup. Translated, 3s. 6d.

The Christian Instructed in the nature and use of Indulgences. By Rev. F. A. Maurel, S.J. 3s.

Protestantism and Liberty. By Professor Ozanam. Translated by W. C. Robinson. 8vo. 1s.

Düsseldorf Society for the Distribution of Good, Religious Pictures. R. Washbourne is now Sole Agent for Great Britain and Ireland. Yearly Subscription is 8s. 6d. *Catalogue post free.*

Düsseldorf Gallery. 8vo. half morocco, 31s. 6d. This volume contains 127 Engravings handsomely bound in half morocco, full gilt. Cash 25s.

Düsseldorf Gallery. 4to. half morocco, £5 5s. This superb work contains 331 Pictures. Handsomely bound in half morocco, full gilt.

"We confidently believe that no wealthy Catholic could possibly see this volume without ordering it for the adornment of his drawing-room table."—*Tablet.* "The most beautiful Catholic gift-book that was ever sent forth from the house of a Catholic publisher."—*Register.*

Catholicism, Liberalism, and Socialism. Translated from the Spanish of Donoso Cortes, by Rev. W. M'Donald. 6s.

The Pope of Rome and the Popes of the Oriental Orthodox Church. By the Rev. Cæsarius Tondini, Barnabite. Second edition. 3s. 6d.

Dramas, Comedies, Farces.

He would be a Lord. From the French of "Le Bourgeois Gentilhomme." Three Acts. (Boys.) 2s.

St. Louis in Chains. Drama in Five Acts, for boys. 2s.
"Well suited for acting in Catholic schools and colleges."—*Tablet.*

The Expiation. A Drama in Three Acts, for boys. 2s.
"Has its scenes laid in the days of the Crusades."—*Register.*

Shandy Maguire. A Farce for boys in Two Acts. 1s.

The Reverse of the Medal. A Drama in Four Acts, for young ladies. 6d.

Ernscliff Hall: or, Two Days Spent with a Great-Aunt. A Drama in Three Acts, for young ladies. 6d.

Filiola. A Drama in Four Acts, for young ladies. 6d.

The Convent Martyr, or Callista. By Dr. Newman. Dramatized by Dr. Husenbeth. 1s.

Garden of the Soul. (WASHBOURNE'S EDITION.) *With Imprimatur of the Archbishop of Westminster.* This edition has over all others the following advantages :—1. Complete order in its arrangements. 2. Introduction of Devotions to Saint Joseph, Patron of the Church. 3. Introduction into the English Devotions for Mass to a very great extent of the Prayers from the Missal. 4. The Full Form of Administration of all the Sacraments publicly administered in Church. 5. The insertion of Indulgences above Indulgenced Prayers. 6. Its large size of type. Embossed, 1s. ; with rims, 1s. 6d. ; with Epistles and Gospels, 1s. 6d. ; with rims, 2s. French morocco, 2s. ; with rims, 2s. 6d. ; with E. and G., 2s. 6d. ; with rims, 3s. French morocco extra gilt, 2s. 6d. ; with rims, 3s. ; with E. and G., 3s. ; with rims, 3s. 6d. Calf or morocco, 4s. ; with rims, 5s. 6d. ; with E. and G., 4s. 6d. ; with rims, 6s. Calf or morocco extra, 5s. ; with rims, 6s. 6d. ; with E. and G., 5s. 6d. ; with rims, 7s. Velvet, with rims, 8s., 10s. 6d., and 13s. ; with E. and G., 8s. 6d., 11s., and 13s. 6d. Russia, antique, with clasp, 10s. 6d., 12s. 6d. ; with E. and G., 11s., 13s. Ivory, 12s. 6d., 16s., 20s., 22s. 6d., and 30s. ; with E. and G., 13s., 16s. 6d., 20s. 6d., 23s. and 30s. 6d. Morocco, with two patent clasps, 12s. Antique bindings, with corners and clasps : morocco, 18s., with E. and G., 18s. 6d. ; russia, 20s., with E. and G., 20s. 6d.

"This is one of the best editions we have seen of one of the best of all our Prayer-books. It is well printed in clear large type, on good paper."—*Catholic Opinion.* "A very complete arrangement of this, which is emphatically the Prayer-book of every Catholic household. It is as cheap as it is good, and we heartily recommend it."—*Universe.* "Two striking features are the admirable order displayed throughout the book, and the insertion of the Indulgences, in small type, above Indulgenced Prayers."—*Weekly Register.*

Some Documents concerning the Association of Prayers, in Honour of Mary Immaculate, for the Return of the Greek-Russian Church to Catholic Unity. By the Rev. C. Tondini. 3d.

The Epistles and Gospels in cloth, 6d., roan, 1s. 6d.

The Little Garden. Cloth, 6d., with rims, 1s,; embossed, 9d., with rims, 1s. 3d.; roan, 1s., with rims, 1s. 6d.; french morocco, 1s. 6d., with rims, 2s.; french morocco, extra gilt, 2s., with rims, 2s. 6d.; imitation ivory, with rims, 3s.; calf or morocco, 3s., with rims, 4s.; calf or morocco, extra gilt, 4s., with rims, 5s.; velvet, with rims, 5s., 8s. 6d., 10s. 6d.; russia, with clasp, 8s,; ivory, with rims, 10s. 6d., 13s., 15s., 17s. 6d.; antique binding, with clasps: morocco, 16s.; russia, 17s. 6d; morocco, with a patent clasp, 10s. 6d.; with oxydized silver or gilt mountings, in morocco case, 25s.

A Few Words from Lady Mildred's Housekeeper. 2d.

"If any of our lady readers wish to give to their servants some hints as to the necessity of laying up some part of their wages instead of spending their money in dressing above their station, let them get 'A Few Words from Lady Mildred's Housekeeper,' and present it for the use of the servants' hall or downstairs departments. The good advice of an experienced upper servant on such subjects ought not to fall on unwilling ears."—*Register.*

Religious Reading.

"Vitis Mystica;" or, the True Vine. A Treatise on the Passion of Our Lord. Translated, with Preface, by the Rev. W. R. Bernard Brownlow. With Frontispiece. 18mo. 4s., red edges, 4s. 6d.

"It is a pity that such a beautiful treatise should for so many centuries have remained untranslated into our tongue."—*Tablet.* "It will be found very acceptable spiritual food."—*Church Herald.* "We heartily recommend it for its unction and deep sense of the beauties of nature."—*The Month.* "Full of deep spiritual lore." —*Register.* "Every chapter of this little volume affords abundant matter for meditation."—*Universe.* "An excellent translation of a beautiful treatise."—*Dublin Review.*

Ebba; or, the Supernatural Power of the Blessed Sacrament. In French. 12mo. 1s. 6d.; cloth gilt, 2s. 6d.

"There are thoughts in the work which we value highly."—*Dublin Review.* "Will do good to all who read it."—*Universe.*

Apostleship of Prayer. By Rev. H. Ramière. 6s.

The Happiness of Heaven. By a Father of the Society of Jesus. Fcap. 8vo. 4s.

God our Father. By the same Author. Fcap. 8vo. 4s.

Holy Places; their Sanctity and Authenticity. By the Rev. Fr. Philpin. With Maps. Crown 8vo. 6s.

"It displays an amount of patient research not often to be met with."—*Universe.* "Dean Stanley and other sinners in controversy are treated with great gentleness. They are indeed thoroughly exposed and refuted."—*Register.* "Fr. Philpin has a particularly nervous and fresh style of handling his subject, with an occasional picturesqueness of epithet or simile."—*Tablet.* "We do not question his learning and industry, and yet we cannot think them to have been uselessly expended on this work."—*Spectator.* ". . . Fr. Philpin there weighs the comparative value of extraordinary, ordinary, and natural evidence, and gives an admirable summary of the witness of the early centuries regarding the holy places of Jerusalem, with archæological and architectural proofs. It is a complete treatise of the subject."—*The Month.* "The author treats his subject with a thorough system, and a competent knowledge. It is a book of singular attractiveness and considerable merit."—*Church Herald.* "Fr. Philpin's very interesting book appears most opportunely, and at a time when pilgrimages have been revived."—*Dublin Review.*

The Consoler; or, Pious Readings addressed to the Sick and to all who are afflicted. By the Rev. P. J. Lambilotte, S.J. Translated by the Right Rev. Abbot Burder, O. Cist. Fcp. 8vo. 4s. 6d., red edges, 5s.

"As 'The Consoler' has the merit of being written in plain and simple language, and while deeply spiritual contains no higher flights into the regions of mysticism where poor and ignorant readers would be unable to follow, it is very specially adapted for one of the subjects which its writer had in view, namely, its introduction into hospitals."—*Tablet.* "A work replete with wise comfort for every affliction."—*Universe.* "A spiritual treatise of great beauty and value."—*Church Herald.*

The Selva, or a Collection of Matter for Sermons. By St. Liguori. 5s.

The Souls in Purgatory. Translated from the French, by the Right Rev. Abbot Burder, O. Cist. 32mo. 3d.

"It will be found most useful as an aid to the cultivation of this especial devotion."—*Register.*

Flowers of Christian Wisdom. By Lucien Henry. With a Preface by the Right Hon. Lady Herbert of Lea. 18mo. 2s.; red edges, 2s. 6d.

"A compilation of some of the most beautiful thoughts and passages in the works of the Fathers, the great schoolmen, and eminent modern Churchmen, and will probably secure a good circulation."—*Church Times.* "It is a compilation of gems of thought, carefully selected."—*Tablet.* "It is a small but exquisite bouquet, like that which S. Francis of Sales has prepared for *Philothea.*"—*Universe.*

A General History of the Catholic Church: from the commencement of the Christian Era until the present time. By the Abbé Darras. 4 vols., large 8vo. cloth, 48s.

The Book of Perpetual Adoration; or, the Love of Jesus in the most Holy Sacrament of the Altar. By Mgr. Boudon. Edited by the Rev. J. Redman, D.D. Fcap. 8vo. 3s.; red edges, 3s. 6d.

"This new translation is one of Boudon's most beautiful works, ... and merits that welcome in no ordinary degree."—*Tablet*. "The devotions at the end will be very acceptable aids in visiting the Blessed Sacrament, and there are two excellent methods for assisting at Mass."—*The Month*. "It has been pronounced by a learned and pious French priest to be 'the most beautiful of all books written in honour of the Blessed Sacrament.'"—*The Nation*.

Spiritual Works of Louis of Blois, Abbot of Liesse. Edited by the Rev. John Edward Bowden, of the Oratory. Fcap. 8vo. 3s. 6d; red edges, 4s.

"No more important or welcome addition could have been made to our English ascetical literature than this little book. It is a model of good translation."—*Dublin Review*. "This handy little volume will certainly become a favourite."—*Tablet*. "Elegant and flowing."—*Register*. "Most useful of meditations."—*Catholic Opinion*.

Heaven Opened by the Practice of Frequent Confession and Communion. By the Abbé Favre. Translated from the French, carefully revised by a Father of the Society of Jesus. Third Edition. Fcap. 8vo. 3s. 6d.; red edges, 4s. Cheap edit. 2s.

"This beautiful little book of devotion. We may recommend it to the clergy as well as to the laity."—*Tablet*. "It is filled with quotations from the Holy Scriptures, the Fathers, and the Councils of the Church, and thus will be found of material assistance to the clergy, as a storehouse of doctrinal and ascetical authorities on the two great sacraments of Holy Eucharist and Penance."—*Register*.

The Spiritual Life.—Conferences delivered to the *Enfants de Marie* by Père Ravignan. Cr. 8vo. 5s.

"Père Ravignan's words are as applicable to the ladies of London as to those of Paris. They could not have a better book for their spiritual reading."—*Tablet*. "A depth of eloquence and power of exhortation which few living preachers can rival."—*Church Review*.

The Supernatural Life. Translated from the French of Mgr. Mermillod, with a Preface by Lady Herbert. Cr. 8vo. 5s.

Holy Communion: it is my Life. By H. Lebon. 4s.

The Eucharist and the Christian Life. By Mgr. de la Bouillerie. Translated. Fcap. 8vo. 3s. 6d.

The Jesuits, and other Essays. By Willis Nevin. Fcap. 8vo. 2s. 6d.

On Contemporary Prophecies. By Mgr. Dupanloup. Translated by Rev. Dr. Redmond. 8vo. 1s.

Good Thoughts for Priests and People; or Short Meditations for Every Day in the Year. By Rev. T. Noethen. 12mo. 8s.

One Hundred Pious Reflections. Extracted from Alban Butler's "Lives of the Saints." 18mo. cloth, red edges, 2s.; cheap edition, 1s.

"A happy idea. The author of 'The Lives of the Saints' had a way of breathing into his language the unction and force which carries the truth of the Gospel into the heart."—*Letter to the Editor from* THE RIGHT REV. DR. ULLATHORNE, BISHOP OF BIRMINGHAM. "Well selected, sufficiently short, and printed in good bold type."—*Tablet*. "Good, sound, practical."—*Church Herald*.

The Imitation of Christ. With reflections. 32mo. 1s. Persian calf, 3s. 6d. Also an Edition with ornamental borders. Fcap. cloth, red edges, 3s. 6d.

Following of Christ. Small pocket edition, 1s. cloth; 1s. 6d. embossed; roan, 2s.; French morocco, 2s. 6d.; calf or morocco, 4s. 6d.; calf or morocco extra gilt, 5s. 6d.; ivory, 15s. and 16s.; morocco, antique, 17s. 6d.; russia antique, 20s.

Conversion of the Teutonic Race. By Mrs. Hope, author of "Early Martyrs." Edited by the Rev. Father Dalgairns. 2 vols. crown 8vo. 12s.

I. Conversion of the Franks and the English, 6s.

II. S. Boniface and the Conversion of Germany, 6s.

"It is good in itself, possessing considerable literary merit; it forms one of the few Catholic books brought out in this country which are not translations or adaptations."—*Dublin Review*. "It is a great thing to find a writer of a book of this class so clearly grasping, and so boldly setting forth, truths which, familiar as they are to scholars, are still utterly unknown by most of the writers of our smaller literature."—*Saturday Review*. "A very valuable work . . . . Mrs. Hope has compiled an original history, which gives constant evidence of great erudition, and sound historical judgment."—*Month*. "This is a most taking book: it is solid history and romance in one."—*Catholic Opinion*. "It is carefully, and in many parts beautifully written."—*Universe*.

Contemplations on the Most Holy Sacrament of the Altar, drawn from the Sacred Scriptures. 18mo. cloth, 2s.; cloth extra, red edges, 2s. 6d.

"This is a welcome addition to our books of Scriptural devotion. It contains thirty-four excellent subjects of reflection before the Blessed Sacrament, or for making a spiritual visit to the Blessed Sacrament at home; for the use of the sick."—*Dublin Review.*

Cistercian Order: its Mission and Spirit. Comprising the Life of S. Robert of Newminster, and the Life of S. Robert of Knaresborough. By the author of "Cistercian Legends." Crown 8vo. 3s. 6d.

Cistercian Legends of the 13th Century. Translated from the Latin by the Rev. Henry Collins. 3s.

"Interesting records of Cistercian sanctity and cloistral experience."—*Dublin Review.* "A casket of jewels."—*Weekly Register.* "Most beautiful legends, full of deep spiritual reading."—*Tablet.* "Well translated, and beautifully got up."—*Month.* "A compilation of anecdotes, full of heavenly wisdom."—*Catholic Opinion.*

The Directorium Asceticum; or Guide to the Spiritual Life. By Scaramelli. Translated and edited at St. Beuno's College. 4 vols. crown 8vo. 24s.

Maxims of the Kingdom of Heaven. New and enlarged Edition. 5s.; red edges, 5s. 6d.; calf or morocco, 10s. 6d.

"The selections on every subject are numerous, and the order and arrangement of the chapters will greatly facilitate meditation and reference."—*Freeman's Journal.* "We are glad to see that this admirable devotional work, of which we have before spoken in warm praise, has reached a second issue."—*Weekly Register.* "It has an Introduction by J. H. N., and bears the Imprimatur of the Archbishop of Westminster. We need say no more in its praise."—*Tablet.* "A most beautiful little book."—*Catholic Opinion.* "This priceless volume."—*Universe.* "Most suitable for meditation and reference."—*Dublin Review.*

The Oxford Undergraduate of Twenty Years Ago: his Religion, his Studies, his Antics. By a Bachelor of Arts. [Author of "The Comedy of Convocation."] 2s. 6d.; cloth, 3s. 6d.

"The writing is full of brilliancy and point."—*Tablet.* "Time has not dimmed the author's recollection, and has no doubt served to sharpen his sense of undergraduate humour and his reading of undergraduate character."—*Examiner.* "It will deservedly attract attention, not only by the briskness and liveliness of its style, but also by the accuracy of the picture which it probably gives of an individual experience."—*The Month.*

The Infallibility of the Pope. A Lecture. By the Author of "The Oxford Undergraduate." 8vo. 1s.

"A splendid lecture, by one who thoroughly understands his subject, and in addition is possessed of a rare power of language in which to put before others what he himself knows so well."—*Universe*. "There are few writers so well able to make things plain and intelligible as the author of 'The Comedy of Convocation.'. . . The lecture is a model of argument and style."—*Register*.

Comedy of Convocation in the English Church. Edited by Archdeacon Chasuble, D.D. 2s. 6d.

Reply to the Bishop of Ripon's Attack on the Catholic Church. By the same Author. 6d.

The Harmony of Anglicanism. Report of a Conference on Church Defence. [By T. W. M. Marshall, Esq.] 8vo. 2s. 6d.

"'Church Defence' is characterized by the same caustic irony, the same good-natured satire, the same logical acuteness which distinguished its predecessor, the 'Comedy of Convocation.' . . . A more scathing bit of irony we have seldom met with."—*Tablet*. "Clever, humorous, witty, learned, written by a keen but sarcastic observer of the Establishment, it is calculated to make defenders wince as much as it is to make all others smile."—*Nonconformist*.

Thy Gods, O Israel. A Picture in Verse of the Religious Anomalies of our Time. Cr. 8vo. 2s.

The Roman Question. By Dr. Husenbeth. 6d.

Consoling Thoughts of St. Francis de Sales. By Père Huguet. 18mo., 2s.

Holy Readings. Short Selections from well-known Authors. By J. R. Digby Beste, Esq. 32mo. cloth, 2s.; cloth, red edges, 2s. 6d.; roan, 3s.; morocco, 6s. [See "Catholic Hours," p. 23.]

St. Peter; his Name and his Office as set forth in Holy Scripture. By T. W. Allies. *Second Edition*. Revised. Crown 8vo. 5s.

"A standard work. There is no single book in English, on the Catholic side, which contains the Scriptural argument about St. Peter and the Papacy so clearly or conclusively put."—*Month*. "An admirable volume."—*The Universe*. "This valuable work."—*Weekly Register*. "A second edition, with a new and very touching preface."—*Dublin Review*.

Sancti Alphonsi Doctoris Officium Parvum—Novena and Little Office in honour of St. Alphonsus. Fcap. 8vo. 1s.; cloth, 2s.; cloth extra, 3s.

The Life of Pleasure. Translated from the French of Mgr. Dechamps. Fcap. 8vo. 1s. 6d.

Sure Way to Heaven : a little Manual for Confession and Holy Communion. 32mo. cloth, 6d. Persian 2s. 6d. Calf or morocco, 3s. 6d.

Compendium of the History of the Catholic Church. By Rev. T. Noethen. 12mo. 8s.

History of the Catholic Church, for schools. By Rev. T. Noethen. 12mo. 5s. 6d.

Benedictine Almanack. Price 2d.

Catholic Calendar and Church Guide. Price 6d.; interleaved, 8d.

Catholic Directory for Scotland. 1s.

Dr. Pusey's Eirenicon considered in Relation to Catholic Unity. By H. N. Oxenham. 2s. 6d.

Familiar Instructions on Christian Truths. By a Priest. No. 1, Detraction. 4d. No. 2, The Dignity of the Priesthood. 3d. No. 3, Necessity of hearing the Word of God. Why it produces no fruit, and how to be heard. On the necessity of Faith. 3d.

Sweetness of Holy Living; or Honey culled from the Flower Garden of S. Francis of Sales. 1s. French morocco, 3s.

"In it will be found some excellent aids to devotion and meditation."—*Weekly Register.*

The Tradition of the Syriac Church of Antioch, concerning the Primacy and Prerogatives of S. Peter, and of his successors, the Roman Pontiffs. By the Most Rev. C. B. Benni. 8vo. 21s., for 7s. 6d.

Père Lacordaire's Conferences. God, 6s. Jesus Christ, 6s. God and Man, 6s. Life, 6s.

Commonitory of S. Vincent of Lerins. 12mo. 1s. 3d.

Men and Women of the English Reformation, from the days of Wolsey to the death of Cranmer. By S. H. Burke, M.A. Vol. i. is out of print. Vol. ii., 6s. 6d.

The chief topics of importance in the second volume are : Archbishop Cranmer's opinions upon Confession ; The Religious Houses of Olden England ; Burnet as a Historian ; What were Lord Cromwell's Religious Sentiments? Effects of the Confiscation on the

People; The Church and the Holy Scriptures; Death-bed Horrors of Henry VIII.; Scenes upon the Scaffold—Lady Jane Grey's heroic Death; The Rack and the Stake; The Archbishop condemned to be Burnt Alive—Awful Scene; A General View of Cranmer's Life.

"It contains a great amount of curious and useful information."—*Dublin Review.* "Interesting and valuable."—*Tablet.* "The only dispassionate record of a much contested epoch we have ever read."—*Cosmopolitan.* "So forcibly, but truthfully written, that it should be in the hands of every seeker after truth."—*Catholic Opinion.*—"On all hands admitted to be one of the most valuable historical works ever published."—*Nation.* "Full of interest."—*Church Review.* "Replete with information."—*Church Times.*

A Devout Paraphrase on the Seven Penitential Psalms; or, a Practical Guide to Repentance. By the Rev. Fr. Blyth. To which is added:—Necessity of Purifying the Soul, by St. Francis of Sales. 18mo., 1s. 6d.; red edges, 2s.; cheap edition, 1s.

"A new edition of a book well known to our grandfathers. The work is full of devotion and of the spirit of prayer."—*Universe.* "A very excellent work, and ought to be in the hands of every Catholic."—*Waterford News.*

A New Miracle at Rome; through the Intercession of Blessed John Berchmans. 2d.

Cure of Blindness; through the Intercession of Our Lady and St. Ignatius. 2d.

BY THE POOR CLARES OF KENMARE.

Woman's Work in Modern Society. 7s. 6d.
A Nun's Advice to her Girls. 2s. 6d.
Daily Steps to Heaven. Fcap. 8vo. 4s. 6d.
Book of the Blessed Ones. 4s. 6d.
Jesus and Jerusalem; or, the Way Home. 4s. 6d.

A Homely Discourse; Mary Magdalen. Cr. 8vo. 6d.
Extemporaneous Speaking. By Rev. T. J. Potter. 5s.
Pastor and People. By Rev. T. J. Potter. 6s.
Eight Short Sermon Essays. By Dr. Redmond. 1s.
One Hundred Short Sermons. By Rev. H. T. Thomas. 8vo. 12s.
Catholic Sermons. By Father Burke, and others. 2s.
The Light of the Holy Spirit in the World. Five Sermons by the Rt. Rev. Bishop Hedley, O.S.B. 1s.; cloth, 1s. 6d.

The Church of England and its Defenders. By the Rev. W. R. Bernard Brownlow. 8vo. 1s. 6d.

Lectures on the Life, Writings, and Times of Edmund Burke. By Professor Robertson. 3s. 6d.

Professor Robertson's Lectures on Modern History and Biography. Crown 8vo. cloth, 6s.

The Knight of the Faith. By the Rev. Dr. Laing.

1. A Favourite Fallacy about Private Judgment. 1d.
2. Catholic not Roman Catholic. 4d.
3. Rationale of the Mass. 1s.
4. Challenge to the Churches of England, Scotland, and all Protestant Denominations. 1d.
5. Absurd Protestant Opinions concerning *Intention*, and Spelling Book of Christian Philosophy. 4d.
6. Whence the Monarch's right to rule. 2s. 6d.
7. Protestantism against the Natural Moral Law. 1d.
8. What is Christianity? 6d.

Abridged Explanation of the Medal or Cross of S. Benedict. 1d.

Diary of a Confessor of the Faith. 12mo. 1s.

Sursum, 1s. Homeward, 2s. Both by Rev. Fr. Rawes.

Sermon at the Month's Mind of the Most Rev. Dr. Spalding, Archbishop of Baltimore. 1s.

Exposition of the Epistles of St. Paul. By the Right Rev. Dr. MacEvilly. 2 vols. 18s.

Commentary on the Psalms. By Bellarmin. 4to. 6s.

Monastic Legends. By E. G. K. Browne. 8vo. 6d.

BY DR. MANNING, ARCHBISHOP OF WESTMINSTER.

The Convocation in Crown and Council. 6d. net.
Confidence in God. Reprinting.
Temporal Sovereignty of the Popes. 1s.; cloth, 1s. 6d.
The Church, the Spirit, and the Word. 6d.

BY THE PASSIONIST FATHERS.

The School of Jesus Crucified. Reprinting.
The Manual of the Cross and Passion. 32mo. 2s. 6d.
The Manual of the Seven Dolours. 32mo. 1s. 6d.
The Christian Armed. 32mo. 1s. 6d.; mor. 3s. 6d.
Guide to Sacred Eloquence. 2s.

Religious Instruction.

The Catechism, Illustrated with Passages from the Holy Scriptures. Arranged by the Rev. J. B. Bagshawe, with Imprimatur. Crown 8vo. 2s. 6d.

"I believe the Catechism to be one of the best possible books of controversy, to those, at least, who are inquiring with a real desire to find the truth."—*Extract from the Preface.*

"An excellent idea. The very thing of all others that is needed by many under instruction."—*Tablet.* "It is a book which will do incalculable good. Our priests will hail with pleasure so valuable a help to their weekly instructions in the Catechism, while in schools its value will be equally recognized."—*Weekly Register.* "A work of great merit."—*Church Herald.* "We can hardly wish for anything better, either in intention or in performance."—*The Month.* "Very valuable."—*Dublin Review.*

The Threshold of the Catholic Church. A course of Plain Instructions for those entering her Communion. By Rev. J. B. Bagshawe. Cr. 8vo. 4s.

"A scholarly, well-written book, full of information."—*Church Herald.* "An admirable book, which will be of infinite service to thousands."—*Universe.* "Plain, practical, and unpretentious, it exhausts so entirely the various subjects of instruction necessary for our converts, that few missionary priests will care to dispense with its assistance."—*Register.* "It has very special merits of its own. . It is the work, not only of a thoughtful writer and good theologian, but of a wise and experienced priest."—*Dublin Review.* "Its characteristic is the singular simplicity and clearness with which everything is explained. . . It will save priests hours and days of time."—*Tablet.* "There is much in it with which we thoroughly agree."—*Church Times.* "There was a great want of a manual of instruction for convents, and the want has now been supplied, and in the most satisfactory manner."—*The Month.*

The Catechism of Christian Doctrine. Approved for the use of the Faithful in all the Dioceses of England and Wales. Price 1d.; cloth, 2d.

A First Sequel to the Catechism. By the Rev. J. Nary. 32mo. 1d.

"It will recommend itself to teachers in Catholic schools as one peculiarly adapted to the use of such children as have mastered the Catechism, and yet have nothing else to fall back upon for higher religious instruction."—*Weekly Register.*

Catechism made Easy. A Familiar Explanation of "The Catechism of Christian Doctrine." By Rev. H. Gibson. Vol. I., 4s. Vol. II., 4s.

A General Catechism of the Christian Doctrine. By the Right Rev. Dr. Poirier. 18mo. 9d.

R. Washbourne, 18 Paternoster Row, London.

A Dogmatic Catechism. By Frassinetti. Translated from the original Italian by the Oblate Fathers of St. Charles. Fcap. 8vo. 3s.

"We give a few extracts from Frassinetti's work, as samples of its excellent execution."—*Dublin Review.* "Needs no commendation."—*Month.* "It will be found useful, not only to catechists, but also for the instruction of converts from the middle class of society."—*Tablet.*

Mgr. de Ségur's Books for Little Children. Translated. Confession; Holy Communion; Child Jesus; Piety; Prayer; Temptation. 3d. each.

The Seven Sacraments explained and defended. Edited by a Catholic Clergyman. 1s. 6d.

Burton's Ecclesiastical History. 1s.

Protestant Principles Examined by the Written Word. Originally entitled, "The Protestant's Trial by the Written Word." *New edition.* 18mo. 1s.

"An excellent book."—*Church News.* "A good specimen of the concise controversial writing of English Catholics in the early part of the seventeenth century."—*Catholic Opinion.* "A little book which might be consulted profitably by any Catholic."—*Church Times.* "A clever little manual."—*Westminster Gazette.* "A useful little volume."—*The Month.* "An excellent little book."—*Weekly Register.* "A well-written and well-argued treatise."—*Tablet.*

Descriptive Guide to the Mass. By the Rev. Dr. Laing. 1s.; extra cloth, 1s. 6d.

"An attempt to exhibit the structure of the Mass. The logical relation of parts is ingeniously effected by an elaborate employment of differences of type, so that the classification, down to the minutest subdivision, may at once be caught by the eye."—*Tablet.*

The Necessity of Enquiry as to Religion. By Henry John Pye, M.A. 4d.; cloth, 6d.

"Mr. Pye is particularly plain and straightforward."—*Tablet.* "It is calculated to do much good. We recommend it to the clergy, and think it a most useful work to place in the hands of all who are under instruction."—*Westminster Gazette.* "A thoroughly searching little pamphlet."—*Universe.* "A clever little pamphlet. Each point is treated briefly and clearly."—*Catholic Opinion.*

The Grounds of Catholic Doctrine. By Dr. Challoner. Large type edition. 18mo. cloth, 4d.

Dr. Butler's *First* Catechism, ½d. *Second* Catechism, 1d.; *Third* Catechism, 1½d.

Dr. Doyle's Catechism, 1½d.

Lessons on the Christian Doctrine, 1½d.

Fleury's Historical Catechism. Large edition, 1½d.
Bible History for the use of Catholic Schools and Families. By the Rev. R. Gilmour. 2s.
Origin and Progress of Religious Orders, and Happiness of a Religious State. By Fr. Jerome Platus, S.J.; translated by Patrick Mannock. 2s. 6d.

"The whole work is evidently calculated to impress any reader with the great advantages attached to a religious life."—*Register*.

Children of Mary in the World. 32mo. 1d.
The Christian Teacher. By Ven. de la Salle. 1s. 8d.
Christian Politeness. By the Ven. de la Salle. 1s.
Duties of a Christian. By the Ven. de la Salle. 2s.
The Young Catholic's Guide to Confession and Holy Communion. By Dr. Kenny. *Third edition*. Paper, 4d.; cloth, 6d.; cloth, red edges, 9d.
Instructions for the Sacrament of Confirmation. 6d.
Auricular Confession. By Rev. Dr. Melia. 1s. 6d.
Explanation of the Epistles and Gospels, &c. By the Rev. Fr. Goffine. Illustrated. 7s.
Rules for a Christian Life. By S. Charles Borromeo. 2d.
Anglican Orders. By the Very Rev. Canon Williams. *Second Edition*. Crown 8vo. 3s. 6d.
Little by Little; or, the Penny Bank. By the Rev. Fr. Richardson. 1d.
The Crusade, or Catholic Association for the Suppression of Drunkenness. By the same. 1d.
Catholic Sick and Benefit Club; or, the Guild of our Lady, and St. Joseph's Burial Society. By the Rev. Fr. Richardson. 32mo. 4d. Burial Society by itself, 2d.
Home Rule. By Rev. Fr. Richardson. 1d.
The Monks of Iona and the Duke of Argyll. By the Rev. J. Stewart M'Corry, D.D. 8vo. 3s. 6d.

Lives of Saints, &c.

Life of the Ven. Anna Maria Taigi. Translated from the French of Calixte, by A. V. Smith Sligo. 8vo. 5s.
Butler's Lives of the Saints. 2 vols., 8vo., cloth, 28s.; or in cloth gilt, 34s.; or in 4 vols., 8vo., cloth, 32s.; or in cloth gilt, 48s.; or in leather gilt, 64s.

Life, Passion, Death, and Resurrection of Our Blessed Lord. Translated from Ribadeneira. 1s.

Oratorian Lives of the Saints. Second Series. Post 8vo.
   Vol. I.—S. Bernardine of Siena. 5s.
   Vol. II.—S. Philip Benizi. 5s.
   Vol. III.—S. Veronica Giuliani, and Blessed Battista Varani. 5s.
   Vol. IV.—S. John of God. 5s.

The works translated from will be in most cases the *Lives drawn up *for* or *from* the processes of canonization or beatification, as being more full, more authentic, and more replete with anecdote, thus enabling the reader to become better acquainted with the Saint's disposition and spirit; while the simple matter-of-fact style of the narrative is, from its unobtrusive character, more adapted for spiritual reading than the views and generalizations, and prologetic extenuations of more recent biographers. The work is published with the permission and approval of superiors. Every volume containing the Life of a person not yet canonized or beatified by the Church will be prefaced by a protest in conformity with the decree of Urban VIII., and in all Lives which introduce questions of mystical theology great care will be taken to publish nothing which has not had adequate sanction, or without the reader being informed of the nature and amount of the sanction. Each volume is embellished with a Portrait of the Saint.

Life of Sister Mary Cherubina Clare of S. Francis, Translated from the Italian, with Preface by Lady Herbert. Cr. 8vo. with Photograph, 3s. 6d.

Stories of the Saints. By M. F. S., author of "Tom's Crucifix, and other Tales," "Catherine Hamilton," &c. 2 vols., each 3s. 6d., gilt, 4s. 6d.

Life of B. Giovanni Colombini. By Feo Belcari. Translated from the editions of 1541 and 1832. with a Photograph. Cr. 8vo. 3s. 6d.

Sketch of the Life and Letters of the Countess Adelstan. By E. A. M., author of "Rosalie, or the Memoirs of a French Child," "Life of Paul Seigneret, &c." 2s. 6d.

Life and Prophecies of S. Columbkille, 3s. 6d.

LIVES OF THE ENGLISH SAINTS.

Life of St. Augustine of Canterbury. 12mo. 3s. 6d.
Life of St. German. 12mo. cloth, 3s. 6d.
Life of Stephen Langton. 12mo. cloth, 2s. 6d.

Prince and Saviour. A Life of Christ for the Young.
By Rosa Mulholland. 6d. Enlarged edition
with extra matter. With 12 beautiful illustrations
in gold and colours. Fcap. 8vo. 2s. 6d.
S. Paul of the Cross. By the Passionist Fathers. 2s. 6d.
Nano Nagle. By Rev. W. Hutch, D.D. 7s. 6d.
Life of St. Boniface, and the Conversion of Germany.
By Mrs. Hope. Edited, with a Preface, by the
Rev. Father Dalgairns. Cr. 8vo. 6s.
"Every one knows the story of S. Boniface's martyrdom, but every one has not heard it so stirringly set forth as in her 22nd chapter by Mrs. Hope."—*Dublin Review.*
Louise Lateau: her Life, Stigmata, and Ecstasies. By
Dr. Lefebvre. Translated from the French by T. S.
Shepard. Fcap. 8vo. 2s.
Venerable Mary Christina of Savoy. 6d.
Memoirs of a Guardian Angel. Fcap. 8vo. 4s.
Life of St. Patrick. 12mo. 1s.
Life of St. Bridget, and of other Saints of Ireland. 1s.
Insula Sanctorum : the Island of Saints. 1s. ; cloth, 2s.
Life of Paul Seigneret, Seminarist of Saint-Sulpice.
Fcap. 8vo., 1s. ; cloth extra, 1s. 6d. ; gilt, 2s.
"An affecting and well-told narrative. . . It will be a great favourite, especially with our pure-minded, high-spirited young people."—*Universe.* "Paul Seigneret was remarkable for the simplicity and the heroism of both his natural and his religious character."—*Tablet.* "We commend it to parents with sons under their care, and especially do we recommend it to those who are charged with the education and training of our Catholic youth."—*Register.*
A Daughter of St. Dominic. By Grace Ramsay.
Fcap. 8vo. 1s. 6d. ; cloth extra, 2s.
"A beautiful little work. The narrative is highly interesting."—*Dublin Review.* "It is full of courage and faith and Catholic heroism."—*Universe.* "One who has lived and died in our own day, who led the common life of every one else, but yet who learned how to supernaturalize this life in so extraordinary a way that we forget 'the doctor's daughter in a provincial town,' while reading Grace Ramsay's beautiful picture of the wonders effected by her ubiquitous charity, and still more by her fervent prayer."—*Tablet.*
The Glory of St. Vincent de Paul. By the Most Rev.
Dr. Manning, Archbishop of Westminster. 1s.
Life of S. Edmund of Canterbury. From the French
of the Rev. Father Massé, S. J. 1s. and 1s. 6d.

The Life of St. Francis of Assisi. Translated from the Italian of St. Bonaventure by Miss Lockhart. With a Preface by His Grace the Archbishop of Westminster. Fcap. 8vo. 4s. gilt.

Life of Fr. de Ravignan. Crown 8vo. 9s.

The Pilgrimage to Paray le Monial, with a brief notice of the Blessed Margaret Mary. 6d.

Patron Saints. By Eliza Allen Starr. Cr. 8vo. 10s.

His Eminence Cardinal Wiseman; with full account of his Obsequies; Funeral Oration by Archbishop Manning, &c. 1s.; cloth, red edges, 1s. 6d.

Count de Montalembert. By George White. 6d.

Life of Mgr. Weedall. By Dr. Husenbeth. 7s. 6d., for 1s.

Life of Pope Pius IX. 6d. Cheap edition, 1d.

Challoner's Memoirs of Missionary Priests. 8vo. 6s.

BY THE POOR CLARES OF KENMARE.

O'Connell: his Life and Times. 2 vols., 24s.

The Liberator: his Public Speeches and Letters. 2 vols., 24s.

Life of Father Matthew. 2s. 6d.

Life of St. Aloysius. 6d.; St. Joseph, 6d., cloth, 9d.; St. Patrick, 6d., cloth, 9d.

Life of St. Patrick. Illustrated by Doyle. 4to. 20s.

Our Lady.

Regina Sæculorum, or, Mary venerated in all Ages. Devotions to the Blessed Virgin from ancient sources. Fcap. 8vo. 3s.

Readings for the Feasts of Our Lady, and especially for the Month of May. By the Rev. A. P. Bethell. 18mo. 1s. 6d.; cheap edition, 1s.

The History of the Blessed Virgin. By the Abbé Orsini. Translated from the French by the Very Rev. F. C. Husenbeth, D.D. With eight Illustrations. Crown 8vo. 3s. 6d.

Manual of Devotions in Honour of Our Lady of Sorrows. Compiled by the Clergy at St. Patrick's Soho. 18mo. 1s.; cloth, red edges, 1s. 6d.

Our Blessed Lady of Lourdes: a Faithful Narrative of the Apparitions of the Blessed Virgin. By F. C. Husenbeth, D.D. 18mo. 6d.; cloth, 1s.; with Novena, 1s.; cloth, 1s. 6d. Novena, separately, 4d.; Litany, 1d., or 6s. per 100.

Devotion to Our Lady in North America. By the Rev. Xavier Donald Macleod. 8vo. 7s. 6d.

"The work of an author than whom few more gifted writers have ever appeared among us. It is not merely a religious work, but it has all the charms of an entertaining book of travels. We can hardly find words to express our high admiration of it."—*Weekly Register*.

Life of the Ever-Blessed Virgin. Proposed as a Model to Christian Women. 1s.

The Blessed Virgin's Root traced in the Tribe of Ephraim. By the Rev. Dr. Laing. 8vo. 10s. 6d.

Litany of the Seven Dolours. 1d. each, or 6s. per 100.

Month of Mary for all the Faithful. By Rev. P. Comerford. 1s.

Month of Mary for Interior Souls. By M. A. Macdaniel. 18mo. 2s.

Month of Mary, principally for the use of religious communities. 18mo. 1s. 6d.

A Devout Exercise in Honour of the Blessed Virgin Mary. From the Psalter and Prayers of S. Bonaventure. In Latin and English, with Indulgences applicable to the Holy Souls. 32mo. 1s.

The Definition of the Immaculate Conception. 6d.

The Little Office of the Immaculate Conception. In Latin and English. By the Very Rev. Dr. Husenbeth. 32mo. 4d.; cloth, 6d.; roan, 1s.; calf or morocco, 2s. 6d.

Life of Our Lady in Verse. Edited by C. E. Tame. 2s.

Our Lady's Lament, and the Lamentation of St. Mary Magdalene. Edited by C. E. Tame. 2s.

The Virgin Mary. By Dr. Melia. 8vo. 11s. 3d. cash.

Archconfraternity of Our Lady of Angels. 1s. per 100.

Litany of Our Lady of Angels. 1s. per 100.

Concise Portrait of the Blessed Virgin. 1s. per 100.

Origin of the Blue Scapular. 1d.

Miraculous Prayer—August Queen of Angels. 1s. 100.

Prayer-Books.

Washbourne's Edition of the "Garden of the Soul," in medium-sized type (small type as a rule being avoided). For prices see page 5.

The Little Garden. 6d., and upwards. *See page* 6.

The Lily of St. Joseph; a little Manual of Prayers and Hymns for Mass. Price 2d.; cloth, 3d.; or with gilt lettering, 4d.; more strongly bound, 6d.; or with gilt edges, 8d.; roan, 1s.; French morocco, 1s. 6d.; calf, or morocco, 2s.; gilt, 2s. 6d.

" It supplies a want which has long been felt; a prayer-book for children, which is not a childish book, a handy book for boys and girls, and for men and women too, if they wish for a short, easy-to-read, and devotional prayer-book."—*Catholic Opinion.* " A very complete prayer-book. It will be found very useful for children and for travellers."—*Weekly Register.* " A neat little compilation, which will be specially useful to our Catholic School-children. The hymns it contains are some of Fr. Faber's best."—*Universe.*

Devotions for Public and Private Use at the Way of the Cross. By Sister M. F. Clare. Illustrated, 1s.; red edges, 1s. 6d.

Path to Paradise. 36 full page Illustrations. Cloth, 3d. With 50 Illustrations, cloth, 4d.

Manual of Catholic Devotion. 6d.; roan, 1s. 6d.; calf or morocco, 2s. 6d.

S. Patrick's Manual. By the Poor Clares. 4s. 6d.

S. Angela's Manual; a book of devout Prayers and Exercises for Female Youth. *Second edition.* 16mo., cloth, red edges, 2s.; Persian, 3s. 6d.; calf, 4s. 6d.

Crown of Jesus. Persian calf, 6s.; morocco, 7s. 6d. and 8s. 6d., with rims, 10s. 6d.; morocco, extra gilt, 10s. 6d., with rims, 12s. 6d.; ivory, with rims, 21s., 25s., 27s. 6d. and 30s.

Burial of the Dead (Adults and Infants) in Latin and English. Royal 32mo. cloth, 6d.; roan, 1s. 6d.

" Being in a portable form, will be found useful by those who are called upon to assist at that solemn rite."—*Tablet.*

In Suffragiis Sanctorum. Commem S. Josephi. Commem S. Georgii. Set of five for 4d.

Paradise of God; or Virtues of the Sacred Heart. 4s.
Devotions to the Sacred Heart. By the Rev. S. Franco. 4s., paper covers, 2s.
Devotions to the Sacred Heart. By the Rev. J. Joy Dean. Fcap. 8vo. 3s.
Devotions to Sacred Heart of Jesus. By the Rt. Rev. Dr. Milner. *New Edition.* To which is added Devotions to the Immaculate Heart of Mary. 3d.; cloth, 6d.; gilt, 1s.
Sacred Heart of Jesus offered to the Piety of the Young engaged in Study. By Rev. A. Deham, S.J. 6d.
Pleadings of the Sacred Heart. By Rev. P. Comerford. 18mo. 1s.; gilt, 2s.; with the Handbook of the Confraternity, 1s. 6d.; Handbook, separately, 3d.
Treasury of the Sacred Heart. With Epistles and Gospels. 18mo. cloth, 3s. 6d.; roan, 4s. 6d.
Little Treasury of Sacred Heart. 32mo. 2s., roan 2s. 6d. calf or morocco, 5s.
Manual of Devotion to the Sacred Heart, from the Writings of Bl. Margaret Mary Alacoque. By Denys Casassayas. Translated. 3d.
Act of Consecration to the Sacred Heart. 1d.
Act of Reparation to the Sacred Heart. 1s. per 100.
The Little Prayer-Book for Ordinary Catholic Devotions. Cloth, 3d.
Missal (complete). Persian calf, 8s. 6d.; morocco, 10s. 6d., with rims, 13s. 6d.; morocco, extra gilt, 12s. 6d., with rims, 15s. 6d.; morocco, with turn-over edges, 13s. 6d.; morocco antique, 15s.; russia antique, 20s.; ivory, with rims, 31s. 6d.
Catholic Hours: a Manual of Prayer, including Mass and Vespers. By J. R. Digby Beste, Esq. 32mo. cloth, 2s; red edges, 2s. 6d.; roan, 3s.; morocco, 6s.
A Prayer to be said for three days before Holy Communion, and another for three days after. 1d., or 6s. 100.
Ursuline Manual. Persian calf, 7s. 6d.; morocco, 10s.
A New Year's Gift to our Heavenly Father. 4d.

Manual of Catholic Piety. Edition with green border. French mor., 2s. 6d. ; mor., 4s.
Occasional Prayers for Festivals. By Rev. T. Barge. 32mo. 4d. and 6d. ; gilt, 1s.
Illustrated Manual of Prayers. 32mo. 3d. ; cloth, 4d.
Key of Heaven. Very large type, 1s. Leather 2s. 6d. gilt, 3s.
Catholic Piety. 32mo. 6d. ; roan, 1s. ; with Epistles and Gospels, roan, 1s. ; French morocco, 1s. 6d., with rims and clasp, 2s.; imitation ivory, rims and clasp, 2s. 6d. ; velvet rims and clasps, 3s. 6d.
Key of Heaven. Same size and prices.
Catholic Piety, or Key of Heaven, with Epistles and Gospels. Large 32mo. roan 2s. ; French morocco, with rims, 3s. ; extra gilt, 3s. ; with rims, 3s. 6d.
Novena of Meditations in Honour of S. Joseph, according to the method of S. Ignatius; preceded by a new exercise for hearing Mass according to the intentions of the souls in Purgatory. 18mo. 1s. 6d.
Novena to St. Joseph. Translated by M. A. Macdaniel. To which is added a Pastoral of the late Right Rev. Dr. Grant. 32mo. 4d. ; cloth, 6d.
Devotions for Mass. Very large type, 2d.
Memorare Mass. By the Poor Clares of Kenmare, 2d.
Fourteen Stations of the Holy Way of the Cross. By St. Liguori. Large type edition, 1d.
Indulgences attached to Medals, Crosses, Statues, &c., by the Blessing of His Holiness and of those privileged to give his Blessing. 1s. 2d. per 100, post free.
A Union of our life with the Passion of our Lord by a daily offering. 1s. 2d. per 100, post free.
Prayer for one's Confessor. 1s. 2d. per 100, post free.
Prayer to S. Philip Neri. 1d. each, or 6d. a dozen.
Litany of Resignation. 1s. 2d. per 100, post free.
A Christmas Offering. 1s. a 100, or 7s. 6d. a 1000.
Intentions for Indulgences. 7d. per 100, post free.
Devotions to St. Joseph. 1s. 2d. per 100, post free.
Litany of S. Joseph, &c. 1s. 2d. per 100, post free.
Devotion to St. Joseph as Patron of the Church. 1d.

Catholic Psalmist: or, Manual of Sacred Music, with the Gregorian Chants for High Mass, Holy Week, &c. Compiled by C. B. Lyons, 4s.
The Complete Hymn Book, 136 Hymns. Price 1d.
Douai Bible. 2s. 6d.; Persian calf, 5s.; calf or morocco, 7s.; gilt, 8s. 6d.
Church Hymns. By J. R. Digby Beste, Esq. 6d.
Catholic Choir Manual: Vespers, Hymns and Litanies, &c. Compiled by C. B. Lyons. 1s.
Prayers for the Dying. 1s. 2d. per 100, post free.
Indulgenced Prayer before a Crucifix. 1d. ea., or 6s. 100.
Indulgenced Prayers for Souls in Purgatory. 1s. per 100.
Indulgenced Prayers for the Rosary for the Holy Souls. 1d. each, 6d. a dozen, 3s. per 100.
The Rosary for the Souls in Purgatory, *with Indulgenced Prayer.* 6d., 8d. and 9d. each. Medals separately, 1d. each, 9s. gross.

Rome, &c.

Two Years in the Pontifical Zouaves. By Joseph Powell, Z.P. With 4 Engravings. 8vo. 3s. 6d.

"It affords us much pleasure, and deserves the notice of the Catholic public."—*Tablet.* "Familiar names meet the eye on every page, and as few Catholic circles in either country have not had a friend or relative at one time or another serving in the Pontifical Zouaves, the history of the formation of the corps, of the gallant youths, their sufferings, and their troubles, will be valued as something more than a contribution to modern Roman history."—*Freeman's Journal.*

The Victories of Rome. By Rev. Fr. Beste. 1s.
Rome and her Captors. Letters collected and edited by Count Henri d'Ideville, and translated by F. R. Wegg-Prosser. Cr. 8vo. 4s.
Defence of the Roman Church against Fr. Gratry. By Dom Gueranger. 1s. 6d.
Personal Recollections of Rome. By W. J. Jacob, Esq., late of the Pontifical Zouaves. 8vo. 1s. 6d.
Supremacy of the Roman See. By C. E. Tame. 6d.
The Roman Question. By F. C. Husenbeth, D.D. 6d.
Henri V. (Comte de Chambord), September 29, 1873. By W. H. Walsh. With a Portrait. 8vo. 1s. 6d.
The Rule of the Pope-King. By Rev. Fr. Martin. 6d.

The Years of Peter. By an Ex-Papal Zouave. 1d.
The Catechism of the Council. By a D.C.L. 2d.
Civilization and the See of Rome. By Lord Robert Montagu, M.P. 6d.
Rome, semper eadem. By Denis Patrick Michael O'Mahony. 1s. 6d.
A Few Remarks on a pamphlet entitled the "Divine Decrees." 6d.

Tales, or Books for the Library.

Tom's Crucifix, and other Tales. By M. F. S. 3s.
"Eight simple stories for the use of teachers of Christian doctrine."—*Universe*. "This is a volume of short, plain, and simple stories, written with the view of illustrating the Catholic religion practically by putting Catholic practices in an interesting light before the mental eyes of children.... The whole of the tales in the volume before us are exceedingly well written."—*Register*.

Simple Tales. Square 16mo. cloth antique, 2s. 6d.
"Contains five pretty stories of a true Catholic tone, interspersed with some short pieces of poetry... Are very affecting, and told in such a way as to engage the attention of any child."—*Register*. "This is a little book which we can recommend with great confidence. The tales are simple, beautiful, and pathetic."—*Catholic Opinion*. "It belongs to a class of books of which the want is generally much felt by Catholic parents."—*Dublin Review*. "Beautifully written. 'Little Terence' is a gem of a Tale."—*Tablet*.

Terry O'Flinn's Examination of Conscience. By the Very Rev. Dr. Tandy. Fcap. 8vo. 1s. 6d.; extra gilt, 2s.; cheap edition, 1s.
"The writer possesses considerable literary power."—*Register*.

The Adventures of a Protestant in Search of a Religion: being the Story of a late Student of Divinity at Bunyan Baptist College; a Nonconformist Minister, who seceded to the Catholic Church. By Iota. 5s.; cheap edition, 3s.
"Will well repay its perusal."—*Universe*. "This precious volume."—*Baptist*. "No one will deny 'Iota' the merit of entire originality."—*Civilian*. "A valuable addition to every Catholic library."—*Tablet*. "There is much cleverness in it."—*Nonconformist*. "Malicious and wicked."—*English Independent*.

The People's Martyr, a Legend of Canterbury. 4s.
Rupert Aubray. By the Rev. T. J. Potter. 3s.
Farleyes of Farleye. By the same author. 2s. 6d.
Sir Humphrey's Trial. By the same author. 2s. 6d.

A Wasted Life. By Rosa Baughan. 8vo. 3s. 6d.
The Village Lily. Fcap. 8vo. 1s.; gilt, 1s. 6d.
Fairy Tales for Little Children. By Madeleine Howley Meehan. Fcap. 1s.; cloth extra, 1s. 6d.; gilt, 2s.

"Full of imagination and dreams, and at the same time with excellent point and practical aim, within the reach of the intelligence of infants."—*Universe.* "Pleasing, simple stories, combining instruction with amusement."—*Register.*

Rosalie; or, the Memoirs of a French Child. Written by herself. Fcap. 8vo., 1s. and 1s. 6d.; extra gilt, 2s.

"It is prettily told, and in a natural manner. The account of Rosalie's illness and First Communion is very well related. We can recommend the book for the reading of children."—*Tablet.* "The tenth chapter is beautiful."—*Universe.*

The Story of Marie and other Tales. Fcap. 8vo., 2s.; cloth extra, 2s. 6d.; gilt, 3s.; or separately:—The Story of Marie, 2d.; Nelly Blane, and A Contrast, 2d.; A Conversion and a Death-Bed, 2d.; Herbert Montagu, 2d.; Jane Murphy, The Dying Gipsy, and The Nameless Grave, 2d.; The Beggars, and True and False Riches, 2d.; Pat and his Friend, 2d.

"A very nice little collection of stories, thoroughly Catholic in their teaching."—*Tablet.* "A series of short pretty stories, told with much simplicity."—*Universe.* "A number of short pretty stories, replete with religious teaching, told in simple language."—*Weekly Register.*

The Last of the Catholic O'Malleys. A Tale. By M. Taunton. 18mo. cloth, 1s. 6d.; extra, 2s.

"A sad and stirring tale, simply written, and sure to secure for itself readers."—*Tablet.* "Deeply interesting. It is well adapted for parochial and school libraries."—*Weekly Register.* "A very pleasing tale."—*The Month.*

Eagle and Dove. From the French of Mademoiselle Zénaïde Fleuriot. By Emily Bowles. Cr. 8vo., 5s.

"We recommend our readers to peruse this well-written story."—*Register.* "One of the very best stories we have ever dipped into."—*Church Times.* "Admirable in tone and purpose."—*Church Herald.* "A real gain. It possesses merits far above the pretty fictions got up by English writers."—*Dublin Review.* "There is an air of truth and sobriety about this little volume, nor is there any attempt at sensation."—*Tablet.*

Cistercian Legends of the 13th Century. Translated from the Latin by the Rev. Henry Collins, 3s.
Cloister Legends: or, Convents and Monasteries in the Olden Time. *Second Edition.* Cr. 8vo. 4s.

Chats about the Rosary; or, Aunt Margaret's Little Neighbours. Fcap. 8vo. 3s.

"There is scarcely any devotion so calculated as the Rosary to keep up a taste for piety in little children, and we must be grateful for any help in applying its lessons to the daily life of those who already love it in their unconscious tribute to its value and beauty."—*Month*. "We do not know of a better book for reading aloud to children, it will teach them to understand and to love the Rosary."—*Tablet*. "A graceful little book, in fifteen chapters, on the Rosary, illustrative of each of the mysteries, and connecting each with the practice of some particular virtue."—*Catholic Opinion*.

Margarethe Verflassen. Translated from the German by Mrs. Smith Sligo. Fcap. 8vo. 3s.; gilt, 3s. 6d.

"A portrait of a very holy and noble soul, whose life was passed in constant practical acts of the love of God."—*Weekly Register*. "It is the picture of a true woman's life, well fitted up with the practice of ascetic devotion and loving unwearied activity about all the works of mercy."—*Tablet*.

Keighley Hall and other Tales. By Elizabeth King. 18mo. 6d.; cloth, 1s.; gilt, 1s. 6d.; or, separately, Keighley Hall, Clouds and Sunshine, The Maltese Cross, 3d. each.

Sir Ælfric and other Tales. By the Rev. G. Bampfield. 18mo. 6d.; cloth, 1s.; gilt, 1s. 6d.

Ned Rusheen. By the Poor Clares. Crown 8vo. 6s.

The Prussian Spy. A Novel. By V. Valmont. 4s.

Adolphus; or, the Good Son. 18mo. gilt, 6d.

Nicholas; or, the Reward of a Good Action. 6d.

The Lost Children of Mount St. Bernard. 18mo. gilt, 6d.

The Baker's Boy; or, the Results of Industry. 6d.

A Broken Chain. 18mo. gilt, 6d.

"All prettily got up, artistically illustrated, and pleasantly-written. Better books for gifts and rewards we do not know."—*Weekly Register*. "We can thoroughly recommend them."—*Tablet*.

The Truce of God: a Tale of the Eleventh Century. By G. H. Miles. 4s.

Tales and Sketches. By Charles Fleet. 8vo. cloth, 2s. and 2s. 6d.; cloth, gilt, 3s. 6d.

The Artist of Collingwood. By Baron Na Carriag. 3s. 6d.

The Convent Prize Book. By the author of "Geraldine." Fcap. 8vo. 2s. 6d.; gilt, 3s. 6d.

Catherine Hamilton. By the author of "Tom's Crucifix," &c. Fcap. 8vo. 2s. 6d. ; gilt, 3s.

Sir Thomas Maxwell and his Ward. By Miss Bridges. Fcap. 8vo. 2s.

Forty Years of American Life. By T. L. Nichols, M.D. 5s.

Catherine grown Older: a sequel to "Catherine Hamilton." Fcap. 8vo. 2s. 6d.; gilt 3s.

Canon Schmid's Tales, selected from his works. A new translation, with 6 original Illustrations. Fcap. 8vo. 3s. 6d.

The Journey of Sophia and Eulalie to the Palace of True Happiness. Translated by the Rev. Father Bradbury, Mount St. Bernard's. Fcap. 8vo. 3s. 6d. ; cheap edition, 2s. 6d.

The Fisherman's Daughter. By Conscience. 4s.

The Amulet. By Hendrick Conscience. 4s.

Count Hugo of Graenhove. By Conscience. 4s.

The Village Innkeeper. By Conscience. 4s.

Happiness of being Rich. By Conscience. 4s.

Margaret Roper. By A. M. Stewart. 6s., gilt, 7s.

Florence O'Neill. By A. M. Stewart. 5s. and 6s.

Limerick Veteran. By the same. 5s. and 6s.

The Three Elizabeths. By the same. 5s. and 6s.

Alone in the World. By the same. 3s. 6d. and 4s. 6d.

Festival Tales. By J. F. Waller. 5s.

Shakespeare's Plays and Tragedies. Abridged and Revised for the use of Schools. 8vo. 7s. 6d.

Poems. By H. N. Oxenham. *Third Edition.* 3s. 6d.

Culpepper. An entirely New Edition of Brook's Family Herbal. Cr. 8vo., 150 engravings, 3s. 6d. ; drawn and coloured from living specimens. 5s. 6d.

The Catholic Alphabet of Scripture Subjects. Price, on a sheet, plain, 1s.; coloured, 2s.; mounted on linen, to fold in a case, 3s. 6d. ; varnished, on linen, on rollers, 4s.

Bell's Modern Reader and Speaker. Cloth, 3s. 6d.

Cogery's Third French Course, with Vocabulary. 2s.

Educational and Miscellaneous.

Horace. Literally translated by Smart. 2s.

Virgil. Literally translated by Davidson. 2s. 6d.

History of Modern Europe. With a Preface by the Right Rev. Dr. Weathers. 12mo. cloth, 5s.; gilt, 6s.; roan, 5s. 6d.

"A work of special importance for the way in which it deals with the early part of the present Pontificate."—*Weekly Register.*

Biographical Readings. By A. M. Stewart. 4s. 6d.

General Questions in History, Chronology, Geography, the Arts, &c. By A. M. Stewart. 4s. 6d.

University Education, under the Guidance of the Church; or, Monastic Studies. By a Monk of St. Augustine's, Ramsgate. 8vo. 2s. 6d.

Elements of Philosophy, comprising Logic, and General Principles of Metaphysics. By Rev. W. H. Hill, S.J. Second edition, 8vo. 6s.

History of England. By W. Mylius. 12mo. 3s. 6d.

Catechism of the History of England. Cloth, 1s.

History of Ireland. By T. Young. 18mo. cloth, 2s. 6d.

The Illustrated History of Ireland. By the Nun of Kenmare. Illustrated by Doyle. 8vo. 11s.

The Patriots' History of Ireland. By the Poor Clares of Kenmare. 18mo. cloth, 2s.; cloth gilt, 2s. 6d.

A Chronological Sketch of the Kings of England and France. With Anecdotes for the use of Children. By H. Murray Lane. 2s. 6d.; or separately, England, 1s. 6d., France, 1s. 6d.

"Admirably adapted for teaching young children the elements of English and French history."—*Tablet.* "A very useful little publication."—*Weekly Register.* "An admirably arranged little work for the use of children."—*Universe.*

Extracts from the Fathers and other Writers of the Church. 12mo. cloth, 4s. 6d.

Brickley's Standard Table Book, ½d.

Washbourne's Multiplication Table on a sheet, 3s. per 100. Specimen sent for 1d. stamp.

Music (*Net*).

BY HERR WILHELM SCHULTHES.

Veni Domine. Motett for Four Voices. 2s. ; vocal arrangement, 6d.
Cor Jesu, Salus in Te Sperantium. 2s.; with harp accompaniment, 2s. 6d. ; abridged edition, 3d.
Mass of the Holy Child Jesus, and Ave Maria for unison and congregational singing, with organ accompaniment. 3s.
The Vocal Part. 4d. ; or in cloth, 6d.
The Ave Maria of this Mass can be had for Four Voices, with the Ingressus Angelus. 1s. 3d.
Recordare. Oratio Jeremiæ Prophetæ. 1s.
Ne projicias me a facie Tua. Motett for Four Voices. (T.B.) 1s. 3d.
Benediction Service, with 36 Litanies. 6s.
Oratory Hymns. 2 vols., 8s.
Regina Cœli. Motett for Four Voices. 3s.; vocal arrangement, 1s.
Twelve Latin Hymns, for Vespers, &c. 2s.

Litanies. By Rev. J. McCarthy. 1s. 3d.
Six Litany Chants. By F. Leslie. 6d.
Ave Maria. By T. Haydn Waud. 1s. 6d.
Fr. Faber's Hymns. Various, 9d. each.
Portfolio. With a patent metallic back. 3s.

A separate Catalogue of FOREIGN Books, Educational Books, Books for the Library or for Prizes, supplied ; also a Catalogue of School and General Stationery, a Catalogue of Second-hand Books, and a Catalogue of Crucifixes and other Religious Articles.

INDEX TO AUTHORS.

Author	PAGE	Author	PAGE
Arnold, Miss M. J.	3	Laing, Rev. Dr.	14, 16, 21
A'Kempis, Thomas	9	Lambilotte, Rev. Père	7
Allies, T. W., Esq.	11	Lane, H. Murray, Esq.	30
Amherst, Bishop	9	M'Corry, Rev. Dr.	17
Bagshawe, Rev. J. B.	15	Macdaniel, Miss	3, 21, 24
Bampfield, Rev. G.	28	Macleod, Rev. X. D.	21
Barge, Rev. T.	24	Manning, Most Rev. Dr.	2, 14, 19
Beste, J. R. D., Esq.	11, 23, 25	Marshall, T. W. M., Esq.	11
Beste, Rev. K. D.	25	Meehan, Madeleine Howley	27
Bethell, Rev. A. P.	20	Mermillod, Mgr.	8
Blosius	8	Milner, Bishop	23
Bona, Cardinal	2	M. F. S.	2, 3, 18, 26
Boudon, Mgr.	8	Nary, Rev. J.	15
Bowles, Emily	27	Newman, Dr.	4
Bradbury, Rev. Fr.	29	O'Clery, Chevalier	3
Browne, F. G. K.	14	O'Mahony, D. P. M.	26
Brownlow, Rev. W. R. B.	6, 13	Oratorian Lives of the Saints	18
Burder, Rt. Rev. Abbot	7	Oxenham, H. N.	12, 29
Burke, S. H., M.A.	13	Ozanam, Professor	4
Butler, Alban	9, 17	Philpin, Rev. Fr.	7
Challoner, Bishop	16	Platus, Fr. Jerome	17
Collins, Rev. Fr.	10	Poirier, Bishop	15
Compton, Herbert	2	Poor Clares	13, 20, 22
Dechamps, Mgr.	11	Powell, J., Esq.	25
Deham, Rev. A.	23	Pye, H. J., Esq.	16
Dixon, Rev. Fr.	3	Ravignan, Père	8
Doyotte, Rev. Père	2	Redmond, Rev. Dr.	13
Dupanloup, Mgr.	4	Richardson, Rev. Fr.	17
Francis of Sales, St.	11, 12	Robinson, W. C.	4
Frassinetti	16	Schulthes, Herr	31
Gibson, Rev. H.	15	Shakespeare	29
Grace Ramsay	19	Shepard, T. S., Esq.	19
Grant, Bishop	24	Sligo, A. V. Smith, Esq.	17
Gueranger	25	Sligo, Mrs. Smith	28
Hedley, Bishop	8	Stewart, A. M.	29, 30
Henry, Lucien	7	Tame, C. E., Esq.	21, 25
Herbert, Lady	3, 7, 18	Tandy, Very Rev. Dr.	26
Hill, Rev. Fr.	30	Taunton, Mrs.	27
Hope, Mrs.	9	Tondini, Rev. C.	4, 5
Husenbeth, Dr.	4, 6, 20, 21	Wegg-Prosser, F. R.	25
Kenny, Dr.	17	Williams, Canon	17
King, Miss	28		

CONTENTS.

	PAGE		PAGE
New Books	1	Prayer-Books	22
Dramas, Comedies, Farces	4	Rome, &c.	25
Religious Reading	6	Tales, or Books for Library	26
Religious Instruction	15	Educational Works	30
Lives of Saints, &c.	17	Music	31
Our Lady, Works relating to	20		

R. WASHBOURNE, 18 PATERNOSTER ROW.